HIDDEN FRUSTRATIONS
by Maureen Mann, M.S., LMHP

Edited by
Malinda Eccarius, M.S.

International Standard Book Number
0-9747889-0-2

Publisher:
Boys Town National Research Hospital
555 North 30th Street
Omaha, NE 68131
402.452.5000 (v/tty)

First Printing 2004
Printed in the United States of America.

DEDICATION

To my parents and siblings and
to my husband and children.

Thank you for your loving support,
patience, and understanding.

ACKNOWLEDGEMENTS

Much appreciation goes to Malinda
Eccarius, BTNRH, who contributed her
time and efforts toward editing this book;
Diane Schmidt, BTNRH, who designed
the cover; Sandy Woods who helped with
proofreading and Dr. Mary Pat Moeller,
BTNRH, for her continuing support
over the years and who made it possible
for me to have this book published.

I want to also thank my family,
colleagues and friends
for believing in me.

FORWARD

Hidden Frustrations chronicles a young woman's remarkable journey of determination. Maureen Mann shares her history as a hard-of-hearing student, striving to learn in mainstream educational settings. She recounts seemingly innocuous school experiences that managed to cut to the core of her self-esteem. She artfully balances these stories with the powerful influences of her parents, her brother, and her husband and children. Their support strengthened her resolve to overcome obstacles of discouragement and led her to a life of helping others remove similar barriers. Maureen helps the reader grasp the subtle effects of a student's feelings of "difference" on self-image and aspirations. Her perseverance appears to arise from personal strength and the loving support of key individuals along the way. She recounts her own formative steps toward self-acceptance, a journey that enabled her to understand and accept her deafness, freeing her to achieve both professional and personal aspirations.

This book is a "must read" for teachers and other professionals working with deaf and hard-of-hearing students in regular education settings. Although much has changed since Ms. Mann went to school, many of her experiences parallel those of contemporary students. Professionals will gain insight from this text about the subtle influences various sources can have on self-esteem. The author provides practical guidance for ensuring that deaf and hard-of-hearing students have access to instruction in the classroom. *Hidden Frustrations* will give parents both guidance and hope. It will help parents understand their children's struggles and triumphs. Most important of all, it will affirm how a family's love and support can be an anchor for the student throughout the school years.

This story has a happy ending. Maureen Mann has become an anchor for an untold number of deaf and hard of hearing students in public schools. She is an exceptional counselor, whose positive approach inspires students to set lofty goals and exceed them. She has the most tender of hearts, and kindness is at her core. This reminds us that it is how one responds to adversity that builds lasting character. I have been along for a good part of Maureen's ride. I have watched her evolve from roles as secretary to classroom aide to professional counselor and national lecturer. She has dedicated herself to each role, striving to contribute in meaningful ways, accepting only the best from herself. Her indomitable spirit is a model to all of us. Her contributions to the field are remarkable; born out of devotion to others and a uniquely determined spirit.

Mary Pat Moeller, Ph.D.
Director, Center for Childhood Deafness
Boys Town National Research Hospital

INTRODUCTION

I was born with a bilateral, moderate to severe sensorineural hearing loss. My brother, Steven, who is two years older than me was born with a bilateral, moderate to severe, sensorineural hearing loss, but his loss became profound by age 15. My mother told me she did not discover my loss until I was four years old, because she thought I was mimicking my brother's speech and I seemed to comprehend well. My parents were surprised by the news because there is no history of deafness in our family. The cause of our hearing loss is unknown. My four other siblings have normal hearing. My parents' reactions were not of sadness or anger. Their attitude was, "Where do we go from here?" They put their energy into what needed to be done rather than wasting their energy over something that could have been. They treated us no differently than the other siblings in terms of how we were raised. The only difference was that we required more time and attention; we needed speech therapy and hospital visits for hearing checkups.

Looking back as an adult, I have more appreciation for how much work and effort they put into making sure we got the most appropriate services possible because they cared for us and loved us. They did not drill us with speech lessons at home but made sure we practiced before we attended our sessions. They did not "mold" us to be "hearing." They had nothing to give us but support, love and respect, even during trying times.

They were just being "parents." I could not ask for more. The other siblings were getting the love and attention as well.

This book was written to help parents and professionals understand my perspective growing up as a person with a hearing loss. Many people think that putting on hearing aids will solve the child's hearing problem. They don't truly understand that it is much more complicated than that. When a hard-of-hearing child goes to school, the primary focus is on the child's academic needs and not on the child's social-emotional needs. I believe that to succeed in mainstreaming, you need to have both. A child who is hard of hearing needs to know he is a part of the school climate and that he feels welcome. He should look forward to going to school every day and he should be treated with respect by his peers and teachers. At times, this is not the case, and we as professionals and parents need to take responsibility to see that the child is happy and has adjusted to his school environment. As a professional counselor and a parent myself, I know that empathy plays an important role. What is it like to be in the hard-of-hearing children's shoes? We don't always take the time to get to know them, to listen to them, to look beyond their hearing aids and their speech difficulties to see that they are truly remarkable people with talents and brains.

My hope is when you read this book, you will have gained some insights and understanding when working with or living with a child with a hearing loss.

"Parents can only give good advice or put them on the right paths, but the final forming of a person's character lies in their own hands." Anne Frank

CONTENTS

CHAPTER 1

EARLY SCHOOL YEARS

My kindergarten year was fun and enjoyable because there was more action than communication. In the beginning, however, I did experience separation anxiety from my mother because I feared the unknown. My teacher was kind and caring and I made friends. From first grade to the seventh grade, I attended a small, parochial school in a small town in Iowa with a population of 500 people. There were three nuns and one lay teacher who taught me. The first year was pleasant as the nun was very kind. I remember one incident during first grade. As I was playing baseball during recess time one morning, I fell on the hard pavement running home from third base. My right knee was badly skinned. The nun came out and soothed me. She took care of me immediately. I remember her warm and gentle touches that made me feel very safe and secure. Little did I know that the feeling of security was not going to last much longer. The nun left after that first year and she was replaced by another nun that taught me in the second and third grade.

This nun did not have much patience with me. To me, she appeared very strict, rigid and with no sense of humor. She always seemed to put fear in me because I never knew when she would get angry. When she did, I never understood why, because I thought I followed the rules and behaved well. At this time, I did not have a hearing aid. She may have been frustrated with me because I probably misunderstood her often. There was one incident that stood out very clearly. We all had to do an assignment in math. The topic was "division." I had no idea what to do with the remainder. When she approached my desk and inspected my work, she immediately yelled at me in front of all the other students, and pulled my right arm back and forth repeatedly until I thought it was going to break off. She did not take the time to explain my mistakes. I did not make the connection that my misunderstanding might be due to my hearing loss. I just figured I was a slow learner in math. It was strange that I never told my parents and I don't know why. I may have felt embarrassed or ashamed. The nun was probably very frustrated too, but that was not the correct way to handle the situation.

During reading times in second and third grade, I remember we all had to take turns reading out loud. I must have had some awareness of my hearing loss. I frequently volunteered to be the first to read. It was difficult to read another student's lips and try to find the spot where he or she was reading, especially if the student was sitting four desks behind me. It was frightening to me when my name was called and I had no idea where to start. I would then be blamed for not paying attention. I was scared of making mistakes because I would be criticized and/or put down in front of the other students. My self image was not off to a good start.

In 1960, and for the next several years, my parents drove my brother Steven and me to a university hospital where we not only sat for several hours waiting for the busy doctors to check our hearing, but also had to be seen by audiologists and a speech pathologist. One does not forget those long hallways, the uncomfortable wooden benches, and the huge clock whose hands would tick very slowly. Our appointment would be at ten o'clock in the morning, and we would finish at six o'clock in the evening. I did not look forward to these yearly visits. I was scared and always seemed to have a lump in the pit of my stomach. I felt different. I thought no one else had to go through this. I still did not quite understand the reason for these earlier visits until finally, at age nine, I was introduced to a hearing aid. I found out years later that I should have received my aid at age six, but there was a communication breakdown among professionals. Little did I know this powerful device was going to remain with me for the rest of my life.

One evening in 1963, two people came to visit my parents. One of them asked me to sit on a piano bench with my back turned to her. She said she would say a word and I was to repeat what she said. I felt good after I finished repeating the ten words. Then, looking at both women and my mother, I could not tell if it was good or bad. After they left, my mother told me the people were audiologists. She said that I had not answered the words correctly. I'm sure my mother tried to tell me something about the hearing aid and that it was coming, but I don't think I understood fully what she meant until a few weeks later when she approached me with a little black box. Inside the box was a funny shaped object with a long cord. When she put the ear mold in my ear, suddenly there were these horrible, loud strange sounds, and I immediately yanked it off. I was familiar, comfortable, and secure with the sounds I had been hearing for nine years. I told my mother that I did not want to wear that ugly thing. She told me that it was a hearing aid and that it would help me to hear better. Unfortunately, for days to come, she had a difficult time convincing me to wear this so called "body aid." I simply was not crazy about its long, awkward cord and the uncomfortable box on my chest.

Hearing aids should have been familiar to me because my brother wore one. However, Steven was my brother and as a kid, I did not think twice about it. I did not pay attention to his aid and did not fully comprehend it. All I knew was when I put the aid on, I felt very different from other people. I no longer felt secure. Who was I? No matter how much support or encouragement I received, beginning to wear a hearing aid at age nine was difficult.

I began reluctantly wearing my new aid to school. Soon after, I recall a most unusual situation in the girls' restroom. While I was sitting on the toilet seat, I heard a "trickling" sound. My first reaction was, "What is this noise?" Where was it coming from? Then it hit me that I could hear my friend going in the next stall. When we were both finished, I told her that the next time she went to the bathroom, she needed to be quieter because I could "hear" her. It was quite embarrassing to me. My friend gave me this strange puzzled look and walked out. I thought I was doing her a favor but obviously I was not.

In fourth grade, I had a lay teacher who was gentle and kind. My favorite place to sit was in the back of the room and not in the front row. I guess I was trying to prove to myself I could function without needing any special help. Everyday before lunch, I would take off my aid and put it in my desk. Trying to be the same as everyone else was very important to my self image. I didn't realize it at the time, but actually, I was hurting myself by not wearing it.

Again, an incident occurred that I will never forget. The girls in the fourth, fifth, and sixth grade classes had to take turns taking lunch count for the lower grades. When it was my turn, I was excited because this position was very important. I took lunch count in my former classroom with the strict nun. I thought I was doing a good job until the following day when she bawled me out in front of the students. She said that the lunch count was incorrect yesterday, and I was not ever to do that again. Her facial expression was stern and her tone of voice was angry. Again, I was humiliated in front of everyone. My younger sister, who was in the first grade class, witnessed the incident. After I left, tears came flowing down heavily and I wet my pants. After that day, I vowed never to take lunch count again. It was not worth the pain and humiliation. I was very angry toward her for putting me through this. It was emotionally damaging. One would think that a teacher would be more sensitive with a child who was hard of hearing. Maybe she finally realized this. My sister told me after that incident, the nun was extra nice to her all day long.

Fourth grade was also the year I started my speech training. My mother would take me and my brother Steven to a city thirty miles away where we received speech therapy from a nice, kind nun. Taking lessons was not always fun and games. As a child, it was hard for me to understand why, like going to the dentist, it was so important to have speech therapy. It was hard to make the connection that speech therapy was important for my future well being. A child lives for the moment, not for the future. Even though I could hear better with the aid, there were sounds that were very difficult to pronounce such as "t", "ch", "sk", "st", "x", and "z." For example, the word "toy" was difficult to pronounce and it took hours of practice to produce a "t" instead of a "k."[1]

I had the same lay teacher for the next two years. I noticed during this time I was starting to have more difficulty with vocabulary. I did not do well on vocabulary tests. Language was becoming increasingly complicated. In order to be a good speechreader, I needed to have good language skills. English was becoming a challenge.

It is true that experts say that the most crucial time for a child to learn language is before age five. By not being fitted with an aid until age nine, I missed a lot of information. Some of the rules in the English gram-

mar were hard for me to comprehend, even
with partial hearing. Therefore, I struggled.
My grades were fair to good during those early
elementary years, but not good enough to pre-
pare me for junior high.

Every year, the students had to take the
Iowa Test of Basic Skills. My scores were always way below average. I remember taking
those scores very seriously and comparing
them with my younger sister whose scores
were very high. Judging from my scores, I
concluded that I was not a very bright child. I
was fortunate that my parents never said a
harsh word about them. They always gave
me support, but it still did not change the way
I felt because I was trying hard to be good at
something. The one positive event I recall
during those years was when I won a spelling
contest in third grade. Spelling was my favorite subject. I also enjoyed reading, even
though writing was a challenge.

Seventh grade was my last year at the
Catholic school. A new church was needed
and it was built on the school site. It was a

relief for me because I did not want my seventh grade teacher, another nun, to teach me in eighth grade. She made sure the aid was in my ear daily before class started and that it stayed there until class was finished. I resigned myself to the fact that she was not going to let me get away with taking it off. She and I had our ups and downs, but she was responsible for teaching me to wear my hearing aid, which would be very important for my future life. At the same time, I was getting support from my family that would make all the difference in my future.

"Children need models more than they need critics." Joseph Joubert

CHAPTER 2

FAMILY LIFE

I grew up on a farm three and one half miles from town. My father was a farmer before he decided to work for the postal services. My mother was a registered nurse for a local hospital. She worked part-time, while at the same time, rearing six children. I was the fourth child and the second child with a hearing loss. I still don't know how she did it to this day, as we children were close in age. Four out of six were born with red hair like their mother. Her parents moved here from Ireland. My father's parents were from German/Irish background. St. Patrick's Day was a yearly celebration!

As a family, we were close knit and we still are. This does not mean my siblings and

I always got along growing up. It seems that at home, at times, I tended to get into trouble or I picked on someone, especially my younger sister because we were only two and one half years apart. My best friend lived not too far from me and we did many things together as if we were sisters. Yet, all in all, we did the typical childhood things; we played with dolls, games, cards and outdoor sports. They were good times!

I don't recall having much difficulty communicating one on one with family members. My parents and siblings were conscientious about talking to my brother and me face to face. However, in large gatherings such as birthday parties, dinners or outside activities where there were more distractions and noises, it was difficult to follow conversations. I remember, at times, my brother sitting quietly at the dinner table because too many people were talking at the same time.

If I missed a question or information about a particular topic, my parents were patient and told me what I needed to know. Not once

do I recall them saying, "Oh, it is not important", or "Oh, it was nothing," or "You don't
need to know that." I never felt shut out unless I didn't ask. They were also good about
filling in the information from television shows.

My mother knew I loved to read. Most
Saturdays when she went shopping, she
dropped me off at the library and I stayed for
two hours reading books and then checking
them out. I also read many plays. I even
wrote my own scripts and had family members act them out.

I joined 4-H in fourth grade and was a
member for nine years. During our monthly
meeting, I hated roll call. I relied heavily on
speech reading. When my name came up, I
had to respond to a question relating to what
the theme was for that meeting. Often, I
missed my name and the question and it was
embarrassing. All eyes turned towards me.
However, if I had worn my aid, it would have
been less stressful. I did not consistently wear
it because I tried to appear as "normal" as
possible, to be liked by all my friends. Some

of those friends did not attend my school. In my mind, they would accept me more as a friend if I did not wear it. The hearing aid continued to be a powerful reminder that I was "different" and I did not want to be a part of that. Being the same as everyone else was very crucial to my emotional well being or so I thought. Little did I know that by not wearing the aid, I was making my life more difficult. It was a real struggle just looking at it. I was not yet ready to deal with it. I wore it during school time because I was told to. That did not mean I accepted it.

One popular game that was often played at 4-H meetings was the "gossiping" game. One person started a sentence by whispering it in another person's ear. That person did the same to her neighbor. This continued until everyone heard it. The sentence had to be the same from beginning to finish. Whenever I played the game, the sentence was never correct. After a few times, when the girls started to eye me, knowing who was not hearing it correctly, I bowed out. I watched from a short distance wishing that I could participate. Even if I had worn the aid, it would not have made any difference. Having someone whispering in my ear was not one of my strengths. I felt so alone. I tended to focus on what I couldn't do instead of what I could do.

Friends during the elementary years treated me well. I grew up with them. My hearing aid did not cause them to perceive me as someone different. However, once we entered junior high, it became a different story.

Because I came from a strong Catholic background, we attended church every Sunday and holiday as well as other special services. I learned to memorize many prayers beginning in first grade. This did not mean that I always understood the meanings behind them. I had the opportunity to play the organ weekly because I took piano lessons and played many songs "by ear" like my mother. How I did that I don't know. Most of my family members are musically inclined.

Playing the organ in church until I graduated from high school was one of my greatest joys, because it was one area where I felt confidence. Before the new church was built, the organ in the old church was in the balcony. One Sunday Mass, I watched for the priest's cue as usual when I was to begin playing. Midway through, I looked over the top of the organ and what did I see? Hands flying about wildly! People, including the priest, were beckoning me to stop because it was not the right time to play. I immediately froze and hid my face! It was a very embarrassing moment. It did not stop me from playing in the future though.

As part of the Catholic religion, my family went to confession monthly. How Steven and I attended at the time was different from the norm. We confessed our sins face to face with the priest because it was difficult to lipread in the dark screened confessional. The priest, of course, could not respond loudly enough. It was not easy to confess my sins in front of him. When I saw my friends going into the confessional, their faces hidden, knowing the priest would not know who was confessing their sins, I felt cheated. Why did my life have to be this way?

My memories with my family, doing things together, getting together with cousins, grandparents, uncles and aunts are happy and fun. We went to many reunions on both sides of the family. My brother Steven and myself had a strong family support system. However, the system was sorely tested at times. At school, where the support system was not strong, we both struggled socially and I struggled myself academically. Junior high and high schools were not always pleasant places to be.

*"The scenes of childhood are the
memories of future years."*
The Farmer's Almanac, 1850

CHAPTER 3

JUNIOR HIGH

Leaving a class of ten to join a class of 138 in a bigger city was not an easy transition. This could be a traumatic experience for any child. For a child with a hearing loss, it was even worse. Most of my former classmates transferred with me. I remember the school building as being dark and gloomy. I felt no warmth or security. There were too many students. I was used to a small class with one teacher for all subjects. In junior high, there were several teachers and each class had at least thirty students. I felt like a number.

A speech therapist was provided for me two times a week. I attended the speech sessions with great reluctance. Why? I did not want to be singled out! The students were very aware of me attending the sessions and I was very uncomfortable with the attention. It was becoming very obvious that I was "different" from the norm. I was also getting tired of continuing lessons and wanted no more of them.

My friends that I had grown up with started to drift away and make new friends except for my best friend from elementary school. In the beginning of the school year, we clung together because they, too, did not know anyone; but when they made new friends, I felt left out. I missed the closeness of my old school where everyone knew me. Now I was among strangers who had not grown up with me and thus, for the first time in my life, I was being teased about my speech, my body aid and my red hair. I was becoming a "people pleaser", trying too hard to win friends. Yet, my way of doing it scared them away.

Some of the boys at school teased me in unkind ways. I had never been teased before and it was a frightening, depressing feeling. My technique was to ignore them and keep my chin up, but ignoring did not always work. It also happened that I was a sensitive child and the slightest remark could hurt my feelings. Another child who is hard of hearing may laugh or joke back and be a good sport about it. I remember I said to myself, "They do not understand, so be patient." Little did I know it was not going to get any better or easier for a long while.

The classes were more challenging and difficult than in elementary school. My grades were very poor. I recall sitting in the front row of each classroom but that did not mean that I understood everything. There were thirty students and a large room means many noises. This was stressful as my aid picked up everything. Speechreading was becoming more challenging. It was difficult to concentrate with noise interference. A question asked from the back of the room would not be repeated by the teacher, and I would miss it. An airplane flying over the school building, the mere sound of a cough or someone crumpling a piece of paper blocked what someone was saying. Being a person who is hard of hearing, I only got a partial sense of what was being said. Many times I guessed. If I caught the first part of a sentence, I would guess what I heard to make it complete. A teacher might write on the board and talk about the topic with his back turned toward me. A teacher might have minimal mouth movement, wear a mustache, cover his mouth with a pencil or a Kleenex, talk while walking up and down the aisle, or stand in front of a glaring window. What could be done when teachers had already been told there was a child who was hard of hearing in the classroom? My mother told me that she talked to all of my teachers. She shared communication strategies with them. Yet, they did not understand. Was it my job to continually remind the teacher? I would not even consider it because I did not want any attention focused on me.

I wish I could say that I enjoyed all my classes. It seems that the teachers did not know how to teach me. One group perceived me as a child who was no different than hearing children. They thought my hearing aid was like a pair of glasses and therefore everything is fine. A hearing aid does not completely correct a hearing loss or always make the teacher audible. Putting me in the front row did not resolve the problem either. The second group's expectations of me seemed low. They saw my hearing aid and decided I was "handicapped" and therefore not very bright. A hearing loss does not mean a student can't think!

The only special treatment I received was sitting in front of the classroom. Nothing extra was done to help create a more comfortable environment for me. Yet, at the same time, language was becoming increasingly complicated and some of the reading materials were difficult to follow. Junior high school vocabulary contained a frightening number of words I had never heard before.

My English teacher was very frustrated with me because of my failure to understand grammar. She tried hard but did not know how to get through to me. Because of my high frequency loss, I wrote only what I heard. I could not hear plural endings. It is difficult for me to distinguish between words such as "different" and "difference" and past tense verbs ending with an "ed" that is pronounced like a soft "t." Words that have soft, unstressed endings are hard to pick up. I remember my oldest brother Leon who tried so hard to teach me. He knew I was having difficulty mastering English skills. I thought the difficulty was all my fault, but my English teacher shared a lot of the responsibility. The important message here is that when a child thinks he failed, it may actually be the teacher's lack of training.

In music class, I remember one particular test where we had to identify the different instruments on a record. Some of the instruments were difficult to distinguish. I received an "F" because I failed to understand the difference. Even though I told the teacher that the reason I looked at another student's paper was because I had difficulty recognizing the sounds, she didn't understand. She thought that because I could speak well, I could hear instruments on a record. I apologized to her for copying but she was upset with me and refused to be sensitive to my plight. I am not sure what it would have taken on my part to convince her that even though I spoke well enough, that did not mean I heard as well. A person who is hard of hearing can be complex. One minute I may hear something right and the next minute, I may be saying "Excuse me?"

Another class was physical education. It was difficult to wear a big body aid and play sports outside. I couldn't hear the teacher well even if I stood up front due to distracting noises like cars going by on the highway. Sometimes the sun blocked her face during a play, making speechreading impossible. The teacher never made any effort to make sure I was following everything she said. Teachers, regardless of whether they have the training or not, should be helpful and show some sensitivity. Some teachers do not have the sensitivity to see that a child needs extra help or emotional support.

Spelling was my best subject and I wanted to enter a spelling bee. I remember looking at the list of words and thinking I could do it. My mother thought I shouldn't participate in this special event because I might not be able to hear some of the words. She advised me not to enter and I followed her advice. Looking back, I understand that what my mother did was not intentional. She wanted to protect me from being hurt. As much as I had been through at that school, another bad experience was not what I needed. If the support system at school would had been stronger, then I would have wanted the challenge no matter what the risk.

My only fond memory of junior high was playing intramural basketball. Emotionally and academically, I was not doing well in eighth grade. Who wanted to be around a child who was being teased constantly? Never in my life had I gotten a C-, D, D+ on my report card or Fs on tests. This did not enhance my self image. During mid-terms, my parents considered another option, a State School for the Deaf. They thought I might do better there and feel a sense of belonging. When I first heard the news, I was depressed. I even remember I was eating my favorite roast beef sandwich from home and I wasn't hungry enough to finish it. I was too close to my parents to want to be separated from them. Being around other children who are Deaf/deaf and hard of hearing was not a pleasant thought to me as I was not one of them. The thought of being sent to a state school would mean "I have failed!" Yet, it wasn't all my fault! The public school had not provided me with what it took for me to succeed. I told my parents I would improve my situation at school. However, my mother did write to the state school to check it out. The superintendent at the time said I was better off in the public school. My mother never completely understood why, but accepted this response. It is possible that I had too much hearing to attend the state school. I was relieved when I did not have to go. I was determined that high school was going to be a much better environment. It could not be any worse than what I had already experienced.

"You never really lose until you stop trying." Mike Ditka

CHAPTER 4

HIGH SCHOOL

I thought high school would improve my social status, but the teasing continued. Because most of the boys who teased me were in a so called "popular clique," other boys were reluctant to ask me for a date or even to be my friends. They didn't want to associate with me when they saw me being teased. Plus, I had to deal with the upper classmen that I had not dealt with before. I was something more of a "tom boy" anyway and preferred playing baseball or basketball to going out on dates. Still, it would have been nice to be invited to homecoming or the prom during my years there.

There was a young male I invited to a hayride party during my freshman year. He

lived in a nearby town and attended another
school. This felt safe to me as he did not know
how I was being treated. He accepted my invitation, to my surprise, and I was thrilled to
death. Maybe there was hope after all. This
person said "yes" to me, a young girl who wore
a body aid, and who continued to struggle with
her self esteem. He was not only handsome
but also popular at his school. The reason I
knew him was because he attended my
church.

The hayride party was sponsored through
our church group. The night of our party did
not turn out to be a major success because it
was difficult to communicate with him in the
dark. While riding in the wagon, my responses
were mostly "yeah" while others were laughing and having a good time. He probably knew
I had a hearing loss. I was too scared and
insecure to tell him. I did not want to ruin
the evening. Ironically, it was ruined anyway
and we never went out again. I did not wear
my hearing aid which did not help the situation. By not wearing it, I felt more "normal."

Yet, I wasn't feeling normal that night, not by a long shot. Had I worn my aid and had a more positive attitude about myself, the outcome might have been different because I think he liked me. Otherwise, he wouldn't have said "yes" to my invitation. Nevertheless, my trust in boys continued to diminish.

At school, walking through the never ending lobbies, the hallways, the classroom, and by tables in the cafeteria, were "smart alec" boys who taunted me and did their best to make me feel uncomfortable and unwelcome at school. It is easy for children to make fun of someone with an unfamiliar disability to assure themselves that they are "normal" and to take the focus off themselves. By doing it in front of children and making it seem okay, they can feel more in control. Little do they know that by doing this to children who may look or act different, they are damaging what little is left of these children's self confidence. By enduring much of the teasing, I survived.

Years later, when I told my mother who was not always aware how bad the situations were, she remarked that my brother and I were born with "tough skins." (Mann, 1991) That may be true but there were times when it became unbearable to go to school not knowing what the day was going to bring. I managed to find a good hideout where the teasers could not get me, the restroom. I spent some time in there for my peace of mind. As soon as the bell rang, I went to my next class.

As I look back, I realized how much control the teasers had over me, to put me in that position. That made me angry and sad. School should be a positive place where one enjoys going and having fun. I wish I had learned some assertive techniques for handling those boys. Looking back, why didn't I confide in an adult? Why did I keep it all bottled up inside me? Didn't any of the teachers notice what was going on? Not always! With so many students to attend to, they must not have noticed what a good job I did covering my feelings. When I started wearing my hearing aid and getting teased, I began to have doubt in myself as a person. Who was I? The stigma attached to the hearing aid signified that I was different, that I was not the same as everyone else. Therefore, was I not normal? I struggled because I knew I was normal. The people that were ignorant about hearing loss did not know any better. How was I to educate them? I did try, but I tried too hard. If no one liked me, how would I like myself? I witnessed some children with other disabilities being teased and I felt for them. Life wasn't fair.

One day during my freshman year, my best friend, whom I have mentioned earlier, and I were riding on the bus together on our way to school. As we were about ready to get off, she turned around and told me she had something to tell me. She said that her older sister had told her that if she continued to be my friend, she would never become popular. Therefore, our friendship was over. This was a devastating blow to me. I had never felt more alone and isolated. I blamed it on my hearing loss. It seemed to have made my life miserable. My self image continued to slide. Every time we saw each other in class or in the hallway, she ignored me. She almost never rode the bus after that. When she did, she completely looked the other way. We hardly ever said anything to each other throughout the rest of our lives.

My brother Steven was not doing so well socially either, but he hung in there with as much pride as he could muster. He loved sports more than anything else. When there was a home high school football game, he was always afraid to go for fear of being taunted. He tried to attend occasionally but it became too difficult. Eventually, he stopped going altogether. Children can be cruel to one another, but to put fear into a child who is hard of hearing and deprive him of having any fun is despicable.

My brother and I did not always share our school problems with each other or with family members. My mother said that we did not talk with her about them. Why, I do not know. My mother worked the three to eleven shift. My father was busy farming so he would get home around nine o'clock at night. When they were home, I probably did not argue as much. With them being there, I felt safe. It may be that we got used to the teasing at school and we put up with it on a day-to-day basis. Or, maybe it was too painful to talk about. However, going home to my brothers and sisters and letting out my anger and frustrations on them made matters worse.

How I was treated at school influenced how I behaved at home. I needed the skills to cope with all the negative environmental feedback I was getting. The inability to cope with the teasing had made me vulnerable. To get rid of the negative feelings, I lashed out at times to my siblings. However, I did not make that connection until years later. At the time, I just thought I was not always a "nice" child, and I wasn't. I wasn't always trying to be mean. I was venting my feelings of anger and frustration to those closest to me, not realizing the harm I was doing to their self image. My parents did all they could to help support me and provide the love they thought my brother and I needed from them. Those times were difficult, but their love and genuine faith in me enabled me to succeed and rise above the obstacles. This did not happen overnight.

My summers during the first three years were spent working at the A&W Root Beer Drive-In as a carhop. I wanted to become independent and earn my own money. I enjoyed meeting people, but at the same time, I feared those groups of boys who came and teased me. I did not let that deter me from working because they didn't come by often. One of the two boys I thought was interested in me was a star basketball player at my school. While I was working one evening, he showed up alone and ordered. As I brought his food to the car, the mustard on the tray tipped over and splashed on his lap. One can imagine the scenario. Whatever chance I thought I had with him quickly faded. He never came back.

During my junior year, there was a big change that made me feel more like a "hearing" person. It was getting a new "behind the ear" hearing aid. It was easier to hide. What a difference it made in my perception of myself! The cord was gone. No more worrying whether the cord was sticking out. No more bulging body aid against my sweating chest. No more big batteries! The body aid was put away forever in it little black box. Yes, life was certainly looking a little bit better or was it?

My speech therapist in high school, Ross Cole, was kind and gentle. He worked with me twice a week on vocabulary. I did not always look forward to seeing him, not because I did not like him, but because of peer pressure. Students made remarks that I perceived as sarcastic, so I did not acknowledge that I was seeing him. Frequently, I would wait in the restroom until the bell rang, and the halls were empty. Then I could go to my speech lesson. There were times though when Mr. Cole came walking in through the front door

and I pretended that I did not see him because I did not want to be associated with
him. I wanted so much to be just "normal."
However, I knew that Mr. Cole genuinely cared
for me and my brother. He always made me
feel I could do anything. He worked hard because he knew I had potential even though I
did not know that at the time.

Every year from the time I graduated until 1986, Mr. Cole sent me and my brother a
Christmas card. When I wrote to him in early
1988 that I did not receive a card from him in
1987, I received a letter from his wife. Mr.
Cole passed away in early 1987 and I grieved.
This was a man who knew I was no different
from anyone else. He treated me and my
brother with the highest respect, which was
rare during our school years. His wife also
mentioned that Steven and I were two of his
best students. Often, we do not appreciate
what is being given to us until years later. It
was too late to tell him how I admired him for
what he did and to thank him. He was a
dedicated man whom I will never forget.

Most classes in high school seemed easier for me than those in junior high. I received better grades. Some of the teachers were nice and some were a challenge. Again, some did not know how to work with me to help me better understand. I probably would not have had to struggle so much if I had someone who understood what I was going through educationally. I recall in a writing class getting papers back marked in red everywhere. However, the teacher never explained why I made those grammatical mistakes. Having them explained to me might have saved me the pain and trouble I faced later in college. Ironically, one would think if the teachers knew my English was poor, they would have taken the time to tutor me. It made me wonder again if their expectations of me were low or whether they felt helpless to teach me. I did not see much effort on their part. The sad part is, I do not recall getting much praise. I do recall, however, receiving criticism for work I did not do well.

There was one class that I took during my junior year that the final exam would determine if I passed. It was given in the cafeteria because the teacher wanted to make sure everyone sat far apart from one another. The students were scattered to limit cheating. I found my place and the teacher walked in. He saw me and did not make any attempt to be close to me while reading the test questions aloud. I felt the burden of responsibility was on me even though he knew I was hard of hearing. It was difficult to speechread him. The acoustics were poor. Considering my time spent studying for the test and knowing my subject well, I felt confident I was going to pass. That confidence quickly vanished as he read the questions. After the test was completed, I approached him in his office. I told him that I felt I did not do well. I could not understand him well enough and had difficulty hearing him with the background noises. His response was, "If you pass, you pass; if you fail, you fail." I was angry and felt helpless. I never thought about "complaining" against him because he was "the teacher." I felt powerless. I almost failed the test and I felt cheated because I studied so hard. I will never forget the teacher's face. It was uncaring, insensitive and cold. He did not have much patience with me. His attitude clearly indicated that not only did he lack sensitivity, but he did not even try to be empathetic. I felt like I was in a "no-win" situation. I later heard that he was also unkind to other students. My hearing loss may not have had anything to do with his attitude towards me.

I had only two friends in high school with whom I socialized, although we were not close. There was one girl who moved to the area in her sophomore area. We might have become good friends but her father moved again a year later. It was tough because I felt she was the first person to accept me with a hearing loss. She and one other friend were the only ones I spent time with outside of school time. Otherwise, my weekends the first three years of high school were mostly spent at home with my family. Every Saturday night, instead of having a date, I watched the "Lawrence Welk Show."

Because I was a pretty good athlete, not surprisingly considering I had two older brothers to play with, I did well in sports at school. In my senior year, I played intramural basketball. Some of the girls that had ignored me the previous years were starting to take notice. "Gee, Maureen is a pretty good volleyball player." In Art class, there was one girl whom I considered the most popular in school because she was kind and funny. There were four students per table. The girl was assigned to my table. Before long, she and I got to know one another and we started to become friends. She perceived me as "Maureen who happens to have a hearing loss." Then her friends started to accept me. For the first time in my life, I was being included. It felt great! I had nothing to hide from them. However, by the time I finally had friends that shared many of the same values, graduation came and people moved on. Going off to college meant to me that I was going to have to start all over again, hiding my aid and not letting anyone know I was hard of hearing. "My self image, always shaky, began wavering like a candle, flicker, dim, flicker, dim." (Mann, 1995) At the same time, my self image in other areas such as playing the organ and playing sports, always there in some degree, had become strong. Without those strengths, I would have been worse off as I completed high school.

During my last year, teasing slowed down but I still didn't get dates. I always felt there were one or two boys that could have been interested in pursuing me but they did not. It could have been the uncertainty, the fear of taking a risk of asking a girl out who wore an aid, or it could have been wishful thinking on my part.

In my final year at high school, I made the honor roll and it was a good feeling. It was a proud moment in my life! My parents attended the banquet with me. Maybe there was hope for me after all! Only time would tell!

> *"You gain strength, courage and*
> *confidence by every experience*
> *in which you really stop to look*
> *fear in the face." Eleanor Roosevelt*

CHAPTER 5

JUNIOR COLLEGE:
LIFE AFTER HIGH SCHOOL

I had not really thought much about going to college or what I would do with my life. My attitude was to make it through each day. All I knew was that my parents wanted me to attend college. They thought it would be good for me to get a higher education, to get a good job. The only strength I thought I had at the time was typing. Therefore, it made sense that I major in medical secretarial science. I chose a medical field because my mother was a nurse. She valued the idea of one of her four daughters becoming a nurse. Having a sensitive stomach however, I told mother this was the best I could do. When I graduated two years later, I found out that I had been on probation for the first six months because of my poor ACT test scores. It was better that I did not know about this until afterwards.

College was a real challenge for me. Part of me was afraid of being alone for the first time even though it was not that far from my home. The responsibilities of being on my own were overwhelming and I threatened to leave several times because of homesickness. If my parents would have said, "Fine, come home to live with us and find a job," I would not be where I am today. Even though I begged and cried for many weekends, they would not yield. They knew I had to be on my own, to grow up. I had to become self-reliant.

Making friends in college was not as difficult as it was in junior high/high school. Yet, I was cautious and did not want to get hurt. Building trust in people was slow. Toward the end of my high school years, I felt like I was slowly coming out of my shell. In college, I was back into my shell again. I did not tell anyone during my first year that I had a hearing loss, but this did not mean that they were not aware of it. It was an issue I felt no one needed to know. Why? Because I was no different from them, but yet I felt different. I was not yet being "me."

The last week of my sophomore year, I decided to go ahead and take the risk of telling one of my closest friends. I wanted to make sure she accepted me for who I was. As I approached her with a lot of courage, I told her there was something very important I had to tell her. She said, "Fine, what is it?" I told her, "I have a hearing loss and I wear a hearing aid." She said, "I know." I looked at her with astonishment and said, "Why didn't you tell me you knew?" She said, "You never asked!" I was thrilled to hear her say that. I realized that someone did like me and I did not have to pretend to be someone I was not, "a hearing person." I felt so relieved not to have to hide it from her anymore! Gradually, I was starting to like myself better, but it was still a slow process. I was not yet ready to tell the whole world.

As far as men were concerned, my memories of them in junior high and high school were still painfully negative. Most men in college treated me like a "sister." Some of them dated my good friends. Again, there was one in a crowd who teased me, but at least it did not hurt my friendship with my female friends. During my two years there, I was dateless. I did invite, which required much courage, two guys from my high school days to go to the prom with me. Neither responded. One can imagine how I felt about men as time went on.

During my freshman year, my mother was asked by a local organization if I would be on a panel which was made up of Deaf/deaf and hard-of-hearing adults. She picked me up at the dormitory. I did not tell any of my friends at the time. I remember running very quickly to the car so no one would notice or ask where I was going. I hid underneath the dashboard as she pulled out. I did not want anyone to find out about my secret.

I am not sure why I volunteered to be on the panel. I guess I did not want to turn my mother down. Reluctantly, I talked about my experience as a person with a hearing loss. I remember feeling very vulnerable, sharing a private secret with people I didn't know. I remember sitting separately at the end of the table, far removed from the rest of the panel members. As soon as it was over, I did not stay to chat with anyone. I waited for my mother in the car. My denial of my hearing loss was still strong and I did not want to be associated with anyone else having the same problem. My experiences so far had been very unpleasant. Seeing a Deaf person using sign language made it all the more painful, a reminder of who I was, and I was not yet ready to face that. My distorted perception at the time was I viewed Deaf people as "handicapped" and I was not one of them.

I remember my first job was answering the telephone in the dormitory. I have no idea how I did it, as I do not do well without an amplification phone. This was probably to show that I was hearing and I was going to do whatever it took to prove that. However, I do recall handing the phone over to various students to take the message when I was having difficulty comprehending. I did this for one year.

College did help me to become responsible and independent although my attitude was still more passive than assertive. I participated in sports, drama, and secretary club. Because my best skill was typing, students would ask me to do their typing. I did a lot of this for free to win friends. After a while though, I felt I was taken for granted and I put a stop to it. I finally became assertive enough to ask for money if anyone wanted their papers typed and it felt good. Typing was the only strength I felt I possessed. I wanted to be the fastest typist in the secretarial department. I practiced typing late every night, including weekends. The purpose was to prove to myself that I could be good at something. I did become the fastest typist, 110 words a minute with no errors. This proved though that with perseverance and hard work, I could reach a goal if I wanted to. It took many hours but it felt good knowing I received positive recognition for it. It also paid off later in future employments.

Academically, I did well in some classes and less well in others. I had some tutoring to help me do better in classes such as Western Civilization. The tests for this course were mainly multiple choice and I have never done well with that. I do much better with essays. Picking which answer best suited the question was always difficult as each choice looked the same to me.

It continued to be a challenge listening in class even while I was sitting up front. I knew I was missing important information by the questions other students asked. For biology, we sat in an auditorium-like room. It was difficult to hear in a big place with everyone spread out. I missed much that was going on. I am sure that affected my grades as test questions were dependent on notes, as well as the textbook. I did not have any notetakers, or any other special help except for tutoring in the one class. I had never even heard of support services. Being stubborn and still in denial did not help, although I did not fully realize the price I was paying for not asking for the help to do better.

Graduation came in May of 1984 and I graduated with average grades. Could I have done better with the proper help such as using a notetaker or a sign language interpreter if they had been available? Yes, I would have but that does not mean I would have accepted them. Remember, I still equated my basic skills test scores and my ACT scores with the idea that I was not a smart student. The subtle signs of low expectations from some of my secondary school teachers (because I was hard of hearing) reinforced my opinion. Sad to say, I do not recall any one particular teacher who said I could do it, who believed in me. Was it the stigma attached to my hearing loss saying, "This is the best I could do?" Only time would tell and it was entirely up to me to believe in myself.

My parents never had doubt in my ability or they would not have persuaded me to go to college. They had faith in me. They wanted all their children to do well. They wanted to give them an opportunity to pursue a career. It was time to be on my own and face the world!

"He who is not courageous enough to take risks will accomplish nothing in life."
Mohammad Ali

CHAPTER 6

LIFE AFTER COLLEGE

After graduation, I was offered a job at a local hospital near the college campus. My job was in the medical records department doing discharge charts. My supervisor was wonderful. However, a year later, she found another job closer to her home and a new supervisor was hired. The new supervisor and I had our difficulties. No matter how hard I tried to get along with her, she seemed to make it her job to find fault with me. One day she told me that I did not hear a physician's order correctly on a particular chart. I told her that I did, but she ordered me to go back to the doctor and check it again. As humiliated as I was, I did and I found out I was correct. When I approached her again, she just shrugged her shoulders and sat down. One can imagine how I felt when I knew I heard it right, but my supervisor thought I misunderstood. Because I have a hearing loss, I did not have as much credibility with her as hearing employees did.

At the hospital, I made new friends. I played softball with them, was on a bowling league and attended many enjoyable parties. My friends knew I was hard of hearing and it made no difference to them. They treated me with respect. My social life was positive and I felt my confidence growing. Teasing was hardly an issue anymore. Something was missing but what was it?

After working for over two years, it was time to call it quits. It appeared that my supervisor clearly did not want me working there. Through the grapevine, I learned that she told someone she did not like working with me because she did not like "deaf people." This grapevine happened to be a very reliable source as she was a very good friend of mine and knew the situation was not getting any better. I decided there was a personality conflict between us. Therefore, it was time to move on. Why should I work for someone who did not appreciate me?

I quit before I found another job. Since it was very difficult to find one, I sheepishly asked for my old job back. The woman in the personnel department said "No." She and the supervisor were good friends so I knew it was hopeless. It was something I should never have done but I had car payments to make. Looking back, I am glad I was turned down. It would have been a step backward for me. The problem would not have gone away between the two of us no matter how hard I tried. I do believe in taking risks and this was one of them. Little did I know what the future held for me. It was meant to be.

I applied for different positions but it was not easy finding a job. My mother's sister was a kind nun. She was also in the Navy for a few years. The Navy sounded like an exciting career so I decided to check it out. I chose the Army instead and took the written test. I passed as they said with "flying colors." I remembered reading that one needs to hear well to join the Army. Believe it or not, even though I told the officers, that I had a hearing loss, they said it did not matter. I thought, "Okay, I will take their word for it." I took a bus with several enthusiastic young people who were anxious to join the Army two hundred miles away. We stayed at the base. We were told we had to be up early the following morning to take different tests that would determine if we passed or not.

There was one handsome young man who rode the bus with me. He asked me out that night and was I flattered! I could not believe my good luck! It was too good to be true. As cautious as I still was, I thought about accepting the invitation; but I finally decided to turn him down because I wanted to be prepared for the next day. Was I crazy? This was my opportunity to have a great time. Either my career was really important or I still did not trust men.

Luckily, during my college days, I had trained my brain to wake me up at a certain time. I did not have a sleep alarm and I could not rely on anyone to wake me up. (I still do this to this day.) When the other recruits and I arrived at the base, there were many people waiting to take the physical tests. I took the eye test and passed. Next was the hearing test. It was a challenge just to hear my name in the noisy room among several people waiting for their turns. After the audio test, the next thing I knew, I was being given a ticket for the bus ride back to my home town. It was humiliating as nothing was kept secret at that base. The people there knew I was immediately rejected.

I waited at the bus station for awhile. I noticed some people that rode with me initially were going to ride back with me. They had passed. The handsome man was one of them. He did not say a word to me all the way home. Again, it was as if I had a disease or something. In the beginning, I felt he treated me as if I was very special. In the end, I felt he treated me as though I were tainted. He may have felt sorry for me and didn't know what to say. One of my friends later said that he may have been embarrassed and avoided me because I first turned him down. That may be quite true. However, as I recall the morning of our testing, we were laughing and talking. He did not seem affected by my turning him down. His attitude took a sharp one hundred and eighty degree turn after I failed the test. He saw it all!

The army officers in my home town found out what happened and wanted me to try for the National Guard. I told them, "Forget it!" My enthusiasm had waned. Eventually, I found a job at the country club, managing a food stand with two younger high school girls. The job paid less than at the hospital, but it was one of the most enjoyable jobs I've ever had. I met many interesting people there. During this time, I seriously considered going back to college. I wanted more than I had.

Because I wanted a job working with people, I decided to become a probation officer. The vocational rehabilitation counselor told me I had to visit several probation officers to see if this was the right career move for me. I will never forget my first visit with her. When she found out I did not sign, she voiced so loud I wanted to turn off my hearing aid. Her mouth movement was so distorted, it made me feel "handicapped." I was surprised by her actions because she had been trained to work with Deaf/deaf and hard-of-hearing individuals. Next, there were psychological and academic tests to be taken. The psychological tests were done in a psychologist's office. The academic parts such as reading, grammar, and vocabulary were done at a local community college.

When the next appointment was held with the vocational rehabilitation counselor, I told her I was still interested in being a probation officer. She said she had received the results from the tests. She stated, "Maureen, you are not smart enough to get a BA degree." Feeling like I was hit in the stomach, I did not know what to say. As stubborn as I was, I was not going to give up without a fight, and I told her I was going no matter what. She reluctantly agreed to help. Remembering her words did not enhance my self esteem. I enrolled that fall at a Catholic college. Within one week, I dropped out because I realized the career I have chosen was not what I thought it would be. Was the VR counselor right? I decided to start looking for another job.

This was a time in my life when I was confused and uncertain what direction I was heading. I did not know what my goals were. I remember taking long walks in the park and getting advice from my older sister and her friends. I moved home to my parents' house and started applying for jobs. I remembered my father having to pay for two car payments and that bothered me. I wanted to be independent. I was hired for two different secretarial positions in two different cities but they did not work out. I quit the one job after one week and the other job after one day. I took both positions without truly understanding what the duties were.

I applied at a university in another city. I took the typing and written tests at the personnel office. To my surprise, I received over thirty offers for secretarial jobs. My scores on the typing test had been very high. I was number one! It was strange to have so many choices. I felt as though God was listening to my prayers. All that hard work at night and during the weekends during my college days had paid off.

The dental secretary job at the University Dental School sounded the most appealing. For almost two years, I worked in the dental production laboratory where I did mostly typing, mailing, receiving and sending dental cases to various labs, and answering the phone. Answering the phone, as you already know, was no easy task for me. I made a different excuse each time such as, "I have a cold, will you please speak up," or "There are background dental noises going on," or "An airplane just flew over." At the time, I did not know about an amplification phone.

I had a great supervisor who knew I was hard of hearing and he was very patient with me. There were three male dental technicians working in the lab and they all treated me with respect too. I felt safe with them. Two were married and one was single. He asked me out several times but I turned him down. We were good friends, but he became frustrated each time I rejected his offer. I never took him seriously because I did not want to be hurt again. I did not know for sure if he knew I was hard of hearing although my supervisor probably told him. From past experience, I was afraid if I told him, it might strain our relationship and I did not want to ruin what we already had. I was still afraid of rejection.

One day, while I was working, my supervisor handed me a sheet of paper which advertised a meeting for anyone who was interested in learning about "hearing impairment." He thought it was important that I attend because he must have sensed that I was restless. Even though I was very happy with my job and my friends, a part of me was saying I

wanted something more out of life. I decided
to go ahead and see what the meeting was
about.

At the meeting, there was a variety of
people such as teachers of the hearing impaired, parents of Deaf/deaf and hard-of-hearing children, interpreters, and people who
were Deaf/deaf or hard of hearing themselves.
I chose not to identify myself. This meeting
reminded me of a sign language class I took
two years after I graduated from high school.
After two sessions, I dropped out. I did not
tell the teacher I was hard of hearing. I took
the class out of curiosity and possibly doing
some soul searching, but it only reminded me
of being different. Being at the meeting and
seeing these people sign made me all the more
confused and depressed. I began to think
about my past, the problems I had faced and
some I had overcome. I left the meeting early.
It was a painful reminder of who I was but it
was also telling me what I needed to deal with.
I knew something had to change but I didn't
have the answer yet. My boss did not say

anything after I arrived back from the meeting nor did I volunteer any information. I was quiet the rest of the day.

One weekend shortly after that, I decided on the spur of the moment to visit my brother Steven who was, at that time, living in northwest Iowa. Perhaps he could provide me with the guidance I needed. Steven was doing well as a teacher for deaf and hard-of-hearing students. He had received his BA degree from the University of Nebraska and a MA degree in Learning Disabilities from the University of South Dakota. Yes, Steven was doing very well and seemed to be happy doing it. I wanted the same contentment. Unbeknownst to me, around the corner, a new chapter in my life was about to begin.

> *"If you could get the courage*
> *to begin, you have the courage*
> *to succeed." David Viscott*

CHAPTER 7

TURNING OVER A NEW LEAF

When I arrived at Steven's school in May of 1978, it was a nice, sunny day. As I approached his classroom, I noticed he was directing several students who were signing and voicing a song called "Sunshine on my Shoulders" by John Denver. I quietly picked a chair in the back of the room and became totally engrossed in their performance. They seemed so happy and content. When I saw how beautiful sign language was, tears started to flow down my cheeks and an inner peace overwhelmed me. At that moment, watching these children made me realize I no longer had to be ashamed of who I was. It took something like this to wake me up and make me face the fact that I was living my life in the shadow of what other people thought or said or what I said to them. So many headaches came from

guesswork, faking, pretending, blaming myself for not hearing it correctly, making as-
sumptions, feeling guilt, shame, self-pity and
even paranoia. This was the turning point of
my life. It was time to just be "me!"

As the song was finished, I asked my
brother if the children were all deaf and hard
of hearing? He said that some of them were
hearing children from another class. They
joined these children for music. I remember
looking at my brother in disbelief and being
dumbfounded. "Are you telling me that they
enjoyed being together? No way!" My brother
explained that the children had known each
other since kindergarten. The hearing children treated them no differently than anyone
else. There was no stigma here. They had
their usual, typical kid's arguments, but otherwise, they all treated each other with respect.
My brother and I felt some sadness that this
has not always been the case for us. However, Steven stated he was happy even though
he went through some difficult times growing
up. My brother's attitude was "past is past."
He lived each day one at a time. My question

to Steven though was "How would your students handle kids that have never been exposed to deafness?" Steven emphasized the importance of learning to confront and solve problems without feeling defenseless or depending on others. The earlier children are given good social skills and empowered with a strong sense of identity, the less they have to struggle throughout their school years.

I admired Steven when he learned sign language while in college although my attitude was "It was not for me but I am happy for you." To me it was a painful reminder that I was different from hearing people and I wanted "normalcy." Yet, denying my hearing loss only added to my frustrations, and those hidden frustrations just grew and grew. Being hard of hearing can be a challenge. Each day can be so unpredictable!

During that weekend, Steven and I had a nice long visit. We talked about what it felt like to be in the middle, between the Deaf and hearing. We both agreed that the teachers we had in school were not trained to teach us. We both agreed that the test scores and college scores were not valid because we were compared to hearing norms, especially since we were not provided with informed educators from the beginning so we could do well on those tests. Our hearing loss affected our English; it was not a reflection of our intelligence. How was I to know that? Did some of the teachers expect that any child with special needs would not have the potential to do well? Did they look first at our hearing loss or at us as human beings? Were we being stereotyped? The only way we could prove our individuality was to believe in ourselves. Steven did. I took a much longer, bumpier route. I was lost along the way but I have finally found the right path. It would be a challenge, but I would not give up. The only person I needed to rely on and to believe in was me.

I will never forget that weekend with my brother. He helped me tremendously. He has many friends, Deaf/deaf, hard of hearing and hearing. One of my favorite stories about him was when he was in a hurry to vacuum his bedroom because his favorite baseball team, the St. Louis Cardinals, was going to be playing on television. He had been in his room for about twenty minutes, but there was no noise coming from the sweeper. I peeked in his room. There he was, vacuuming away while the sweeper was unplugged. When I showed the plug to him, his face became beet red. He was too distracted about the upcoming game to think about the vibration of the sweeper. I told him I should have let him sweat it out for another twenty minutes because it was fun watching him vacuum.

I attended a Deaf function with my brother shortly after my visit with him. It was the Midwest Athletic Association for the Deaf (MAAD). Even though my signing was not even at the basic level, I was warmly accepted. It was a great feeling!

That same fall, I enrolled in an interpreter training program. My goal at the time was to be a medical interpreter. I realized my limitations in being an interpreter in a group, but I could do one-on-one interpreting. However, my first goal was to learn all I could about my hearing loss as well as learning sign language. There were some people who thought the program might be too difficult for me, but they were not associated with the program itself. One gets tired of hearing the word "can't." My attitude now was "I can." I had some reservations, but I was ready for a real challenge and no one was going to stand in my way. It was hard saying good-bye to all my friends when I moved.

Socially, during those two years at the dental school, I had made many nice friends. Some knew I had a hearing loss; some did not, or so I thought. It was an issue that was rarely discussed. However, there was one time when I did discuss it with a male dental student. He came in my office one day and said his grandmother had a hearing loss. He sat down and talked with me about it. I remember he was very nice and sweet to me. I was surprised by his sincere attitude as it was rare for any male friends to discuss this openly with me.

My friends and I went disco dancing at least three times a week. Dancing was fun even though I knew my hearing could be affected by the loud music. There were some men I met there and dated, mostly students from the University. There were always parties going on. My dates were not very successful. When I was testing my self image, I bravely told one date I was hard of hearing and he immediately dropped me like a "hot potato."

My brother Steven set up a blind date for me with his good friend. At first, I was reluctant to accept this offer because Steven's friend was deaf and I was not comfortable with the idea of dating a deaf man. I agreed because I trusted my brother. We went out to eat and had a nice visit but I remember feeling uncomfortable. The next time I talked with my brother, he said that his friend thought I was nice but did not want to go out with me again. After hearing this, I felt relieved.

I then decided it was too painful to admit, as it seemed from my experience, men did not accept me for the person I was. I got along fine with the men I did not date. They were either married, dating someone else or had a working relationship with me.

I was looking forward to a new journey in my life, meeting new friends and turning over a new leaf. Would there be a young man in my future who would capture my heart?

"I want to be all that I am capable of becoming." Katherine Mansfield

CHAPTER 8

A NEW JOURNEY

Participating in the two year interpreting program was the best decision I have ever made. The teachers were great! One of them was a Deaf leader in the community, Joe Myklebust. I learned so much from him and we became very good friends. Joe was also my inspiration. He was truly one of the most remarkable men I have ever met. He passed away in 1985 and I miss him.

Getting into the interpreter training program was like a big step into the unknown; a truly different path than I had ever experienced. My life up until then had been in the hearing world. I tried so hard to act like a hearing person. Now I was taking a risk, making myself vulnerable by sharing with

people that I am hard of hearing. I found myself stepping forward, then taking two steps
backward, forward, backward etc., until I
gained more and more confidence in myself.
I was slowly letting go of the past but only in
bits and pieces. Seeing something familiar
would bring up an unpleasant memory.

One incident was the day I had to return
a book to the library. I saw a group of boys
standing next to the outside door and talking. All of a sudden, I remembered a similar
scene back in high school where a group of
boys sat together in the high school cafeteria
together, making fun of me as I passed them
by. I saw such a group more than once and
I would wait by the car until the group broke
up. Slowly though, I began to change my
thought process. "These are not the same boys
as in high school. They will not tease you."
After I began to walk by a group of young men,
whether it was in the cafeteria, library, a car,
my confidence began to grow. My attitude
then shifted to "So what if they do tease me, it
does not matter to me anymore. The problem

is theirs, not mine." However, teasing was never a problem at college. The paranoia I had felt before began to disappear. I was on my way to healing. The negative teasing did leave a big scar and I wanted to get rid of it. It is not good to keep negative feelings buried. Letting the feelings of bitterness and anger remain buried can affect one's relationships and ability to trust others. I did not want any of that. I wanted to change who I was and it was going to happen!

The psychology course on deafness helped me to understand the problems from my past. Piece by piece I was starting to unravel the puzzle of why I acted the way I did. My anger and sadness were due to my frustration with not knowing how to deal with the problems I had in school. I had not related my angry outbursts at home to being teased at school. The more I understood the reasons for some of my inexcusable behaviors and why I acted that way, the more I found peace within myself. For example, when a boy teased me about my speech, I ignored him. When I arrived home from school, I was already upset and then got into a fight with my younger sister. My sister did not understand because I did not understand.

"I had to learn to forgive. That meant forgiving myself as well as others who either, through lack of knowledge or lack of sensitivity, had hurt me while I was a vulnerable child. To heal we must first deal with why we are angry at ourselves and others before we can overcome anger." (Mann, 1995) I also asked for forgiveness from those I have hurt. I chose to move forward because I wanted to become my own person.

I received extra help during my time at the interpreting program. I took a speedreading course. I received extra help in English and writing as I had never really received proper help from a trained person who understood how to work with Deaf/deaf and hard-of-hearing students. What a difference it made in my ability to comprehend difficult reading assignments! The extra help during this time spared me frustration later in getting my higher degrees.

During an audiology course, we tested children with hearing loss at the nearby state school for the Deaf. It was fun to be on the other side, doing the testing, when all these years it had been me in the soundproof room. It helped me to understand my earlier experiences.

The only time I ever felt left out in one of my classes was when I could not sign a song from a record or interpret from a tape recorder, but I accepted it. I knew it was something I could not do because I have a hearing loss. There was no more of feeling sorry for myself. It was important to be realistic and focus on the strengths I had.

During the two year interpreting program, I learned a lot about myself. I learned American Sign Language, the language of the Deaf. At first, I remember being uncomfortable and I was not sure what I was getting myself into.

It was not the stigma attached to it because that was gone. I think it was more a question of "Could I do it?" However, the feeling went away quickly once I started to learn more about it and began enjoying it. Ironically, I graduated with high honors. This is something I never thought would happen, but I was clearly trying to prove that I could do it.

I received a letter from a counselor from my junior high days. I did not know her very well, but she wrote me a congratulatory letter on my achievement. I was surprised by this letter. It made me wonder why I did not get the support at the time I needed it. She probably had no idea because I did not ask for it.

What does it take to believe in someone? Must having a hearing loss be an obstacle? Does a student's hearing loss prevent some professionals or significant others from setting high and realistic expectations? I think many people were surprised by my achievement. My brother Steven was a role model and an inspiration. To see that he fulfilled his dream of being a teacher for the Deaf/ deaf and hard of hearing only motivated me all the more to pursue my goals. I was lucky to look up to someone and see that he could do it. If he can, so can I!

I worked part-time as a residential advisor at the school for the Deaf. It was not the first time I set foot in the place. When my brother was getting his BA in deaf education, he did his internship at the same school. When my family visited him one weekend, I went along to see where he taught. I remember that I reluctantly got out of the car. Steven was proud to show where he was working. All of a sudden I saw a group of Deaf children clustering around him and enjoying his presence. I could see he was truly a role model for them. All I remember saying was "That's nice, that's nice" and then I went back to the car.

Who could imagine I was going to work here at the very place I had not wanted to acknowledge five years earlier? It was a good experience working there for two years. I learned a lot, especially when I saw that these children were no different than me. Socially, they had something I did not have. I had no peers other than my brother to identify with my hearing loss. I felt isolated. It was the identity that was missing. It was the emotional part that was lacking. These children perceived their deafness as a cultural issue, not a medical issue. Most of them did not struggle with their identities.

The first time I attended the Deaf club, I was apprehensive. Even though I was warmly welcomed at the Midwest Athletic Association of the Deaf, there was still some fear of rejection when I went to the Deaf club, a fear that I may not fit in. The fear quickly dissipated when Joe, my teacher, greeted me. He introduced me to his friends. Again, this was an emotional time for me. I began to feel that I belonged in a world I had rejected earlier in my life because of my denial. They did not judge me even though I had judged them without ever personally knowing them. I did not grow up in their culture. American Sign Language was not my native language. However, we shared a common bond that could not be described in words. The feeling of mutual understanding was there. I was their friend and they were mine. It was wonderful to feel that I belonged.

Before I joined the interpreting program, my attitude was to go to school and study. There was no time to meet men and I had no desire to do so. Well, that certainly changed sooner than I thought. Of the six of us that graduated, one was a man named David. David became interested in taking the program because he grew up with a Deaf neighbor. They became good friends but communicated mostly via fingerspelling. By joining the program, David would be able to communicate better with his friend and become a professional interpreter. He was also working part-time at the school for the Deaf and for NAPA Genuine Parts Company.

A few months later, I was to find a partner to do a Christmas song together. Walking back to my dorm one day, I saw David sitting in a lounge, doing laundry. He beckoned me to come in. As I approached him, he asked me to be his partner and I said "Yes." Every day after that, we met in the library and just signed about anything. We went with a group of Deaf people to basketball games, Deaf club and out to eat. Then one day, he asked me out and I said "Yes" cautiously. I still did not trust men very well and I was not about to get hurt again. I kept my distance. The funny thing was David was cautious too because he had broken up with a girl he dated for three years and planned to marry. It took him a year to get over that. Therefore, we were both playing it safe. He already knew I was hard of hearing and it did not matter to him. I did not have to hide it from him. He still liked me for who I was. Two and a half years later, David asked me to marry him under an old oak tree at my parents' farm. He told me, "When God made you, he threw the mold away." After hearing this, I was numbed.

What could I say? No one ever had said such kind words to me. I felt that David was the first person to truly love me for who I was, not rejecting me because I was hard of hearing.

During the summer of 1979, David and I went to Gallaudet College, now known as Gallaudet University, the only liberal arts college for the Deaf/deaf/hard of hearing in the world. We both took advanced classes in American Sign Language. Attending this college was an honor for me. I was becoming more involved in the field of deafness and my curiosity never waned. It felt right.

One thing I always wanted to do during my younger years was to be on stage and perform. Feeling like an outcast and being shy, I never tried out for a play. In third grade I was given one line "So that's how the wind blows." The audience actually laughed at what I said and it felt good. However, I was not brave enough to try out during my high school years. As a sophomore in college, I did participate in the play "The Devil and Daniel Webster." I had lines as well as dancing with a partner. It was enjoyable. I was good at memorizing because I was taught that way during my earlier years at the Catholic school.

I heard many great things about the National Theatre of the Deaf (NTD) summer program. I was determined to apply for admission even though I had limited acting experience. During the spring of 1979, I applied and told a few people. Some of them said, "Forget it!" When I saw the thin envelope waiting to be opened, sadly I knew I had not been accepted. However, that did not deter me from trying again and I applied the following year. When I saw the thick envelope, I knew I was accepted. That summer was one of the most exciting times in my life. I learned so much about acting, directing, fencing, ballet, jazz, and clowning, to name a few. Meeting interesting people from all over and spending a day in New York City to see the Broadway play, "Children of a Lesser God" was like a dream come true for me. I, Maureen Green, was in a beautiful place called Waterford,

Connecticut, learning all I could about the beauty of signing in drama and poetry, and meeting fascinating instructors and actors who knew their crafts well. Again, it is something I will always cherish as it was a goal I wanted to accomplish. I made many good memories there and I have pictures to prove it. I made this happen! Acting was fun and I seriously thought of doing it as a career. However, I decided on a more stable vocation and that was being a teacher for the Deaf/deaf and hard of hearing. I also wanted to be close to David.

The fall of 1980, I enrolled in an elementary education program. When I asked for assistance from the vocational rehabilitation counselor, he gave me his respect and support. He believed in me! He also saw that I had the confidence to further my education. After taking classes for two months, I decided this was not what I wanted. I did not share the enthusiasm about becoming a teacher that I saw other students display. A part of me knew I was good at listening to people and being empathetic. Therefore, I changed my major from elementary education to psychology. My goal was to become an agency counselor. Because I utilized both a notetaker and a sign language interpreter, I received my BA degree in the winter of 1981 without much difficulty.

There was one thing I wanted to do. It was to locate the first vocational rehabilitation counselor who told me I was not smart enough to receive a BA degree. I found out she had moved on to a different city. I wanted to show her my degree and tell her she was wrong about me. What would have happened to me if I had listened to her? How many professionals are out there giving poor advice to those who want to pursue their dreams? How many untrained psychologists are misinterpreting test results? I found out that the vocational rehabilitation counselor had become blind. I let it rest.

My goal in becoming a counselor was to help others realize their potential and to be all they could be. The next step was to find a graduate program in the field of agency counseling.

> *"If you can imagine it, you can achieve it.*
> *If you can dream it, you can become it."*
> *William Arthur Ward*

CHAPTER 9

WHAT'S NEXT?

Coming back from the NTD summer program, I needed a job. There was an advertisement in the newspapers for a secretary/ interpreter position at Boys Town Institute which is now known as Boys Town National Research Hospital (BTNRH). I thought, "With my secretarial and interpreting background, I will check this out." The interpreter position was mainly one on one. My typing was still fast and I got the job. My boss gave me the chance to prove myself. One thing that she did was write everything in long hand because she knew how difficult it would be for me to hear her voice on a transcribing machine. I stayed with this position for less than ten months as I felt the stress of going to college and working full time. I decided on a part-time position at the hospital as a child care technician. In other words, I was a teacher's aide for a group of children who were deaf and hard of hearing. Those kids today are now graduating from high school. How time flies! I loved this position and had it for three years before I got my master degree. It was a lot of fun.

I got married the summer of 1981 before I finished my Bachelor of Arts degree. It was a year that three of my siblings got married. Everyone's wedding was beautiful. Mine was held at the Dowd chapel on the Boys Town campus, a beautiful Cathedral with stained glass windows. All my friends, Deaf/deaf, hard of hearing and hearing were there to witness my marriage to David. There were two sign language interpreters to interpret the wedding. I also signed a song "Evergreen", from "A Star is Born" to David. August 22nd was a gorgeous day with all my wonderful friends and family.

During those three years, from the time I had turned over a new leaf in 1978, until I got married in 1981, I had made more friends than I thought possible. The best feeling was they all knew who I was and I still mattered to them. I found out who my true friends were and they accepted me unconditionally. I was thankful that I did not waste my life in bitterness and pretending that I was "hearing." I was truly happy and content being "me" without shame. This did not mean my life was going to be without challenges, but at least I was moving forward in the right direction. It was time to educate people to get rid of the myths, stereotypes, and the stigmas attached to being Deaf/deaf or hard of hearing.

Getting into the counseling program was a challenge. Filling out the application form and following up with what I needed to do were not the problems. The question from one professor was "Can you do this?" Again, I had to prove I could do it. During a group interview for admission, I brought my interpreter because hearing in a group was difficult for me. It was not easy to watch everyone, not knowing who was going to speak next. The counselor in charge of the group told me that he wanted me to read his lips and not use the interpreter. He was not familiar with how to utilize an interpreter. I told him the purpose of the interpreter's presence but he was not about to give up. Again, he stated he wanted me to read his lips. I was flabbergasted that this counselor was giving me a hard time. I stood my ground and told him I needed to use this interpreter to understand everything. I realized then and there that I needed to become better at being assertive consistently. Learning how to be more assertive became easier as my confidence grew. My advisor was empathetic because he had a progressive hearing loss which occurred during his later years. He helped me a lot and he believed in me. He allowed me to take some classes from Gallaudet University which were related to deafness.

Two years later and a week after I took the four hour counseling examination, I had a baby girl, Colleen Ann. David and I were happy because we wanted to start a family. From what I understood during delivery, the doctor almost dropped her and the nurse caught her! Later that night as I slept, a nurse woke me up and said that Colleen needed a blood transfusion. I asked the nurse what was wrong and I did not have my hearing aid on immediately. I was frightened as the first thing that popped into my head was that Colleen was not going to make it. The nurse wanted me to sign a paper. After putting the aid on, I asked the nurse the same question, "What is wrong with Colleen?" She knew I was upset and instead of telling me what the problem was, she told me to wait until I talked with the doctor. However, the doctor didn't show up until much later. He told me that Colleen was anemic and therefore needed blood. There was a breakdown in communication. This confusion could have been avoided had I educated the staff more about hearing loss rather than just saying "I am hard of hearing."

I still find myself doing the full work load of reminding people that I am hard of hearing. It would be nice if other people were better informed about hearing loss so that I would not always have to make that extra effort.

However, if I want clear communication, to know what is going on, I am going to have to be responsible initially, especially with new people. If I do not, then they speak to me as though I were a hearing person. It is much easier to say "I am deaf" because then other people will change their communication strategies.

Getting my Master of Science degree in agency counseling a month after Colleen was born was a proud moment for me. I have gained many insights from the counseling courses I have taken. Books I have read on assertive techniques, empowerment, and how to be a better communicator have also enhanced my self esteem.

For those who did not believe in me, I am very glad I believed in myself. How many people took advice seriously from those who said they couldn't do it and thus never fulfilled their dreams? I am so glad I listened to myself, however long it took. There have been barriers but I have conquered them.

Staying home for the next six months with Colleen was fun. At first, I was overwhelmed by the responsibility of taking care of a small baby. However, that quickly changed and being a new mother was something I was looking forward to.

"Your success and happiness lie in you." *Helen Keller*

CHAPTER 10

FIRST PROFESSIONAL JOB

I clearly recall assuring myself several times that I would never live in three cities in Iowa that were previously associated with my hearing loss. The memories of speech training made me avoid the first city even though I graduated from a junior college there. I didn't like the second city because I went to the University hospital there yearly for hearing and speech tests. Yet I lived and worked there for two years. They were happy times. The third city I wanted to avoid was where the state school for the Deaf is located, and yet that area is still my home today. After taking a break for six months with my newborn daughter, Colleen, I received a call to work at Boys Town National Research Hospital as a mental health counselor working with abused chil-

dren with disabilities. I would work in this
field for almost nine years. The hospital made
sure that communication was accessible for
me. I utilized an interpreter at staff meetings, professional meetings and conversations
with the police and social workers, to name a
few. Counseling abused children and their
families was stressful but rewarding. I served
not only this diverse group but also hearing
clients as well. This gave me a wealth of experience I could use later to serve clients with
many different disabilities.

During those nine years, I worked with
Deaf/deaf, hard of hearing and hearing professionals. It was a good learning experience
for me. Because it was time for me to move
on, to expand my skills, I transferred over to
another department at BTNRH called the "Center for Childhood Deafness." In my new role,
I worked with families whose infants and tod-
dlers were Deaf/deaf or hard of hearing. For
three years, I ran a parent support group at
the hospital on a weekly basis. I also continued my expertise as a counselor in serving

Deaf/deaf and hard-of-hearing clients at the hospital.

At the present time, I am one of three counselors providing counseling services for three different school districts. BTNRH contracts with the school districts to provide services for Deaf/deaf and hard-of-hearing students, ranging from preschool to high school, such as individual, group and family therapy and seminars for staff. It has been a wonderful experience thus far. I also teach sign classes and I am an evaluator for educational interpreters. All of this keeps me rather busy!

Since the National Theatre of the Deaf summer program in 1980, there has been no time for me to continue with acting. I have done artistic interpreting for social functions such as weddings, theaters and Deaf organizations. During the fall of 1996, I took an acting class at the Omaha Theatre Playhouse. In May of 1998, I decided to take a risk and audition for a play with Deaf and hard-of-hearing actors. I played the role of "M'Lynn" in a play called "Steel Magnolias" performed at the Diner Theatre in Omaha. It was a lot of fun. It was done in American Sign Language. Since then, I have performed leading roles in several plays. The actors have been hearing, Deaf and hard-of-hearing. The experience of these plays was wonderful. I also did a national and local commercial and they were fun but hard work. Again, this shows that one can achieve anything! It will happen if one makes it happen! The important thing is I took the risk. The more I believe in myself, the more I take risks. I believe it is important to set goals and follow through with them.

Since Colleen, I have had two more children, Ryan and Sean. Both are a joy! Shortly after Sean was born, I noticed I was not hearing as well. After being tested at BTNRII, I learned that my hearing loss progressed from moderately severe to profound. When I was told about this, it felt weird because all these years my hearing has been stable. It is okay though because now I have an identity. I was told that my giving birth to Sean may have triggered the drop.

As for raising children, it is a challenge everyday but a rewarding one. David and I have been married for 22 years. The secret of our successful marriage is keeping communication open and having respect for one another. It is nice to be able to trust my husband and feel secure.

We are busy with our children's activities. I let my children know that I am not ashamed of being deaf/hard of hearing. If I am not ashamed, they will not be embarrassed either. I have many sentimental stories to prove this but I will share just two with you.

When Colleen was nine years old, she came home from school one day with a manila folder. Inside were music sheets. I asked, "What is this?" Colleen said, "I asked my teacher to give me copies of the songs we are singing for an upcoming concert so you can follow along with us." I remember the tears flowing. How sensitive Colleen was to include me. My feelings were overwhelming. She wanted me to enjoy the music with her as I was a part of her world too. Since then, my sons have carried on with this tradition.

During the spring of 1996, my son Ryan's class did a song in sign language. My husband went to school weekly to teach them the signs so they could perform. As I sat on the bleachers, again I was overwhelmed with emotions. I said to myself, "This is too awesome!" My son, his class, my husband, the music teacher, the audience of parents and others saw this happening. I was at a loss for words. I was included in this small community and not just an outsider looking in. What progress I have seen here in my own children carrying out the message that signing is beautiful since the day I sat down and watched my brother's students signing the song, "You Are My Sunshine." My attitude helped all of this to happen. I would never have dreamed this could happen. If I had continued on my original path, I would never have experienced any of this. How blessed I was to have that conversation with my brother who was my inspiration 25 years ago. I am blessed to have Deaf/

deaf/hard of hearing and hearing friends. But most of all, I am blessed that I have found my self respect.

> *"All our dreams can come true, if we have the courage to pursue them."*
> *Walt Disney*

CHAPTER 11

PERSONAL VIEWS

TEENAGE YEARS

Professionals working in the field of education need to understand and be trained to work with Deaf/deaf and hard-of-hearing students. There was no outside consultant during my youth to work with teachers. There were no itinerant teachers. There are schools out there today that still do not think the hard-of-hearing children have special needs. The issue that is often overlooked is, "We are not hearing!"

A hearing aid is not a substitute for "hearing." "Imagine the noise all day long at school, in the hallway, cafeteria, and classroom. Talk about stress! The stress of having a hearing loss is continuous. It never goes away. People who are hard of hearing never know from one minute to the next what factors will make fluent communication impossible." (Mann, 1991) There were difficult materials to understand. Listening to the teachers day in and day out and trying to stay focused was terribly challenging. This is what I call "hidden frustration"; the frustration of not only dealing with teasing but also trying to comprehend communication on a daily basis.

Some high school students, whether they wear or do not wear their hearing aids, complain of headaches and being exhausted when they get home from school. Their eyes are strained from too much concentration on lipreading.

"Many people who are hard of hearing do a lot of guesswork or faking because they may feel too embarrassed to ask questions. They do not want to draw attention to themselves, be singled out, or be reminded that they are hard of hearing. There may be a feeling of shame. There is a desire to be the same as everyone else. The frustration is there. The hidden frustration from ineffective communication is overwhelming unless the hard-of-hearing child receives support from those around him or her. The frustration building inside can lead to behavioral problems." (Mann, 1991)

"The teenage years are a crucial and difficult time when many things happen such as body changes, mood swings, identity confusion, strong desires for peer approval, and the struggle for independence from parents. Being a teenager is a challenge in itself. Adding a disability, such as a hearing loss, makes being a teenager even more difficult." (Mann, 1991)

"Peer approval is very important during the teenage years (i.e, the desire to be the same as everyone else, to wear the same designer clothes and hairstyle, to talk the same way, to be part of a popular crowd, to be part of something, in other words, "to be hearing."

Imagine being the one teenager in the entire school who talks "funny," who watches people's lips to understand, and who wears a hearing aid behind the ear. The hearing aid is a powerful symbol that reminds the hard-of hearing-teenager that he/she is different. When one is being ridiculed, other students do not want to be associated with the person who is hard of hearing because they do not want to be teased as well. Students tease other students who are a little different because they are unfamiliar, uncomfortable with, or unac-cepting of any differences." (Mann, 1991)

"Being a teenager can be stressful. One will try very hard to fit in by hiding the hear-ing aid, not asking questions in class, not drawing attention to himself or herself, not volunteering to share information in case someone else said it, or volunteering to be first to avoid embarrassment and frustration. Be-ing the only student who is hard of hearing in the entire school is a common occurrence. Therefore, the teenager who is hard of hear-ing has no one else with whom to identify, no peer or older role model. A stigma is attached to the hearing aid that signifies "I am not hearing, so who am I?" This leads to identity confusion." (Mann, 1991)

Too often, professionals focus on the academic needs of the child and not enough on the social/emotional needs. To be successful in mainstreaming, a child who is hard of hearing must balance a good self image with academic achievement. To have both requires a strong network of people working together to make the child's adjustment positive. (Mann, 1991) This includes parents, the community and the school. (Froehlinger, 1981) If one of the support system is absent, then the child's self image may suffer.

Hard-of-hearing students who go to the state school for the Deaf go for different reasons. Some hard-of-hearing students do well academically but not socially. At the state school, they have found their sense of belonging. They may consider themselves a part of the Deaf community.[2] Their parents may allow their hard-of-hearing teenager to make the decision regarding placement. They want their child to be happy, to fit in.

Some hard-of-hearing students failed academically in the public schools and were sent to the state school for the Deaf. Some of them do not adjust to this environment either. They may not consider themselves as part of the Deaf community. Socially, they had friends from their previous schools but the focus of adults was academic.

Some hard-of-hearing students struggled both socially and academically in the public schools and were sent to the state school for the Deaf. They may or may not adjust to this environment.

Some hard-of-hearing students, whose parents are culturally Deaf, choose to go to the state school for the Deaf because they identify with the Deaf community.

There are other hard-of-hearing students who were sent to the state school for the Deaf because they were considered to have bahavioral problems. Why? Were their educational needs being met? Did they have additional learning problems? Did they have friends? Did we listen to their feelings? Maybe the hard-of-hearing students felt no one truly understood what they were going through and crucial decisions were made as to where they did belong. Yet, did we solve their problems?

Are we too quick to brand them as "failures"? What are we not doing to provide an appropriate education for these students? What kind of an environment are we providing for them? What are the factors needed to allow hard-of-hearing students to succeed academically and socially in the mainstream schools? Professionals and parents are still trying to answer these questions.

Vira Froehlinger, editor of a book called *Today's Hearing-Impaired Child: Into the Mainstream of Education*, provided a list of factors she felt that contribute to successful mainstreaming. They are as follows:

1.   Setting appropriate educational goals;

2.   The child's self confidence and self esteem;

3.   Child's communication ability;

4.   Cooperative and committed parents;

5.   Positive teacher attitude and commitment

6.   Expanded teacher skills;

7.   Hearing peers' understanding and acceptance;

8.   Shared philosophy;

9.   Good administrative leadership;

10.   Positive school climate;

11.   Appropriate curriculum and learning materials.

12. Interagency cooperation; and

13. Community readiness. (Froehlinger, 1981)

Additional suggestions that come from Froehlinger's book, as well as my personal experiences, are as follows:

1. Socialization with peers (Deaf/deaf, hard of hearing and hearing)

2. Involvement in school activities;

3. Qualified educational interpreters/ notetakers;

4. Including the hard-of-hearing students in some of the decision-making. We need to do a better job of listening to them.

Unfortunately, I don't always see this implemented. Of course not every school district understands the needs of the hard-of-hearing students, but it is also true that some of these factors are not being utilized because not every school is committed. If, for example, an administrator of the school is not committed, that can be felt among some teachers and thus they have the same attitude. Some of these professionals have been employed a long time and do not like changes, even to benefit the child who is hard of hearing. This is why parents must be active as the child's advocates. If not, then the child will have a difficult time succeeding. Those who do consider some or all of these factors, i.e., parents, teachers, administrators, counselors, interpreters, and the students themselves are the people who work together to make it happen. It is so important that we all treat these students with respect. They then will respect you.

SIGN LANGUAGE

I often hear that sign language is not necessary for people who are hard of hearing, whether for academic or communication purposes. Suppose that 25 years ago there had been educational sign language interpreters. Would my expository writing papers have been covered with red ink? Would I have struggled less with English? Would my language have been enriched? Would my scores on the Iowa Test of Basic Skills and the ACT have been higher? Would I have been a better communicator?

Sign language, in my opinion, is not only for people who are Deaf/deaf. Hearing people do not have to wear hearing aids from morning until night and hear amplified noises for the rest of their lives. At times, hard-of-hearing children need to be given permission if they ask to take their aids off during recess and after school for play. Some students prefer not to always wear them during physical education. There are many of us who like the quiet and who can concentrate better playing ball without the added distractions.

Hard-of-hearing children may have Deaf/deaf or hearing parents. Some hard-of-hearing students (with hearing parents or deaf parents who were raised orally) who have graduated from high school, wish they had learned sign language during their school years for academic, social and emotional reasons. The feeling of belonging is so important. They wish they had been introduced to other hard-of-hearing, Deaf/deaf children even if they did not attend their schools. The sharing of that identity is quite powerful. "I understand you and you understand me." No explanation is needed. We need to stop and think that some hard-of-hearing children may be more comfortable having friends who are Deaf/deaf, and hard-of-hearing as well as hearing. By socializing with peers who have hearing losses, their sense of identity may not be quite as confused.

There are some hard-of-hearing children who are born to Deaf parents. Some of them, like hard-of-hearing children of hearing or deaf parents, also experience the feeling of "Where do I belong, in the hearing or Deaf world?" There are deaf families where parents do not consider themselves as culturally Deaf. However, other hard-of-hearing children with Deaf parents may perceive themselves as culturally Deaf because they identify with their families and have been raised primarily in the Deaf community.

I believe there are no harmful effects when hard-of-hearing children learn sign language. It is helping, not hindering many children's communication development. It can help, rather than hinder children's reading and writing skills. It can help, rather than hinder the child's receptive communication. It can help, rather than hinder a child's emotional well being and self image. The acceptance and understanding of adults provide hard-of-hearing children with all possible resources to enrich their growing years with language through auditory and visual means.

Some hearing parents have shared with me that their hearing children learned sign language when they were babies. Children can produce signs a few months before they can produce spoken words. My children learned sign language before they spoke. How wonderful it is for them to be able to communicate so early with their hands. Speech came but the interaction was already established between the children and their parents. They had already experienced success in using language symbols to connect with the most important people in their world, their parents, very early in life.

Yes, I would have struggled less if I had had more visual support. Sign language does not hinder speech for most children. It helps bridge communication. However, communication is the goal. I have seen children trying to converse orally with their parents and professionals only to be interrupted and told they pronounced a word wrong and to please say it again correctly. What is more important? Communicating ideas and feelings or correcting a word or a speech sound? What does it do to the child? Articulation can be corrected at a more appropriate time and place.

We need to be careful not to stereotype all hard-of-hearing children as doing well by only using auditory/verbal modes of communication. Some do well and others do not. It can be frustrating when I see many hearing professionals making decisions about what is best for a hard-of-hearing child when they don't have enough information. It is important to focus on the uniqueness of the child. Too often parents obtain information from professionals who are biased. They do not provide all of the options available and allow the parents to choose what they think is best for their child. Perhaps we, as professionals, could do a better job if we asked advice from those who had real experience with hearing loss as children, the hard-of-hearing adults themselves.

Most hearing people use English as their language. Most people who are Deaf use American Sign Language, commonly known as ASL. Yet, there are deaf children and adults who communicate using a spoken English or an English system of signs. For people who are hard of hearing, why can't they have access to both spoken English and Sign Language?

As I look back on my life, I know it would have been easier if I had received early intervention prior to age five, if I had utilized a qualified educational interpreter, notetakers and/or assistive listening devices as a supplement to speech and hearing aids, if I had associated with Deaf/deaf and hard-of-hearing peers and role models and if my support system, both academic and social/emotional, at my schools had been stronger. Yet, most of these services were not available for me during my early years.

There are hard-of-hearing children today who have succeeded because they utilized these resources. Others may get only part of the assistance they need. We need to focus on the individual strengths and needs of each hard-of-hearing child. If the child is not doing well socially and emotionally, this could become one of the goals in the child's Individual Educational Plan (IEP). However, I have seen many IEPs that seem to reflect only academic components and not the social and emotional aspect of the child's development. We need to look at both components to enable the child to succeed. Everyone in the child's support system needs to work together as a team. They need to remember they are discussing the child's future. Most hard-of-hearing children who are now adults will be able to tell you vividly who helped them in school and who did not. They will remember who inspired them and who discouraged them.

HEARING AID USAGE

As a counselor, I have counseled some hard-of-hearing students who refused to wear their hearing aids or FM devices at school for several reasons. Perhaps they did not want to be singled out or teased; maybe the hearing aids were uncomfortable or made them feel different. I have seen students who do wear hearing aids and may or may not be struggling with their self esteem. However, I have also seen some of them wearing hearing aids while utilizing sign language interpreters. Hearing aid use may or may not be an identity issue. Sign language may be their preferred communication mode in the classroom but not socially. It is important in each case to explore the impact of hearing aids on their academics and social interaction.

There are some hearing students in junior high who are "cruel" to hard-of-hearing students. I have heard "teasing" stories about their speech and hearing aids and it breaks my heart. I remember one hard-of-hearing teenager who told me, "I kept looking into my invisible bag of tricks to find a way of coping with the teasing until my hand kept getting deeper in the bag. One day, the bag was empty." The teenager ran out of ideas and became frustrated.

I know exactly what these students are going through and I feel for them. It would be very easy for me to take care of their problems, but it would not teach them to help themselves. As a counselor, I can teach them the skills they need to handle teasing, listen to their feelings, build their confidence, help them feel good about themselves and let them know they do not "own" the problem. I have done "sensitivity classes" and we do roleplaying. The hard-of-hearing students themselves share their feelings. As a counselor, I have discovered that personality plays a role in determining what coping strategies might be used by a particular child.

Often, parents and professionals wait until the child gets into junior high before they call me and say they have a problem with their

child not wanting to wear his hearing aids.
The problem can go back to as far as first
grade. It is easier to handle the problem when
they are younger. The challenges ahead may
be easier to handle if one doesn't wait until
they get into junior high/high school. High
school is already a challenge for any child. It
is even more challenging when you don't have
the support of some teachers and parents.
They don't understand what hearing aids can
do and why it is important for the hard-of-
hearing student to wear them daily and not
inconsistently (especially when they don't have
any other mode of communication such as
sign language). Yet, for some parents, hearing aids are not important because the families have other priority issues they need to
deal with in their lives, and we need to appreciate that. When that happens, we as professionals need to do our best to help the child.

We need to educate teachers and administrators. We also need to educate the hard-
of-hearing students about their hearing loss.
We need to empower them. Then they can
educate their friends in the classroom, even

demonstrating their hearing aids, cochlear implant or FM trainer. This can eliminate any misconceptions other children may have about people with hearing loss. Hearing aid related communication issues also need to be addressed with teachers. All of this can help provide a smoother road ahead for the hard-of-hearing child. Of course there will always be challenges, but we can do a lot in the way of prevention that can save headaches later. We need to educate yearly because there are always new students and new teachers.

There are some people who say that elementary hard-of-hearing students can make their own decisions about whether they want to wear their hearing aids. As I look back to when I was in seventh grade, if I had been allowed to make my own decision, I would have chosen not to wear it. I had worn it off and on prior to that but the nun's decision was to make me wear it daily. Suppose she had let me make the decision. How would that have affected my grammar, reading and writing in high school? In college? How would that have affected my social life? My social-emotional development? My self esteem? My speech? How would that have affected my becoming an adult? My career? Would I have had more problems? More obstacles? One thing I know for sure is my life would have been more challenging!

After wearing my hearing aid in junior high, I knew I had to wear it in high school. This did not mean I accepted it. However, I knew it was my link to communication.

Some hard-of-hearing students say they do not want people to notice that they are wearing hearing aids. Yet, by not wearing them, they are bringing more attention to themselves. They say "What?" a lot and avoid conversing with peers in small groups unless they are in control of the conversation. They don't truly understand that they are making it tougher on themselves. I think elementary school age students (and even some older students) do not have the cognitive ability or mature understanding about the importance of wearing hearing aids and the impact it will have on them throughout their lives to make that decision.

I remember one high school hard-of-hearing senior who was a cheerleader. She was from out of state. She was struggling with her self esteem and did not wear a hearing aid. (She did not know sign language.) Her parents wanted her to wear it but she said her audiologist told her she did not have to. Thus, it became a struggle between herself and her parents and she came to see me. She said that she had lots of friends in school and she didn't think they would accept her if she wore her hearing aid. I asked her, "If they won't accept you as who you are, are they your friends to begin with?" She thought about that. I told her that they probably knew she had a hearing loss and she was making it harder on herself. Her friends didn't seem to have a problem with this. The problem was how she perceived herself. The biggest issue was that she was not being herself and not liking herself for who she was. A couple of years later, she sent me a letter saying she wanted to become a counselor.

Parents and professionals need to take the responsibility for seeing that the elementary hard-of-hearing students are wearing their hearing aids consistently. Of course, flexibility is important. One young fourth grader complained to me and said he has to wear his hearing aids from the time he gets up until he goes to bed. At times, he wants some peace and quiet. I jokingly said to him, "Well, I don't think you wear them in the shower do you?" He said, "I take a four minute shower! That is not long enough!" I agreed with him. There needs to be some compromising.

Strategies need to be implemented to help students feel comfortable about wearing the hearing aids rather than forcing them to wear them. They need to get used to hearing sound and feeling ear molds in their ears. Parents can allow them (depending on age) to decide on the color of the ear molds or the plastic casing for their hearing aids. Again, we need to give hard-of-hearing students some control. If the students are or are not wearing their hearing aids and struggling with their self-esteem, I work with them on the underlying issues.

More and more schools are eliminating the body trainers with the long cords (one wears it in front) and opt for the "boot," (direct audio input) which is an attachment to the hearing aid. The teacher wears the microphone. Most hard-of-hearing students don't like the body FM units because they really make them "stand out." When one student got a new "boot," he felt ten times better. What a difference it makes in how they feel. They like to blend in with the other children. Unless one is hard of hearing, one does not truly understand or appreciate how it feels to wear a body trainer, cochlear implant, or hearing aids. Parents' and professionals' attitudes, support and knowledge can go a long way to help shape these children's lives for the better.

COCHLEAR IMPLANT

There are children with severe to profound hearing loss who have cochlear implants. A cochlear implant is a surgically implanted electronic device designed to provide auditory stimulation. Children and or adults who receive the implants do not benefit from hearing aids. Some children with cochlear implants utilize sign language as their primary mode of communication and others rely primary on auditory/verbal communication.

With ever increasing technology, in a few years we may see more children with cochlear implants functioning as hard of hearing. My concern is for those children who will be mainstreamed in rural areas. Will they have an identity? Will they experience the same social isolation and loneliness that I did? Who is going to nurture their self esteem? Will they have the support they need to succeed? Are we there for these children today? These are some questions we need to think about. We must never lose sight of the fact that despite their cochlear implants, these children are still not hearing individuals nor should they be treated as such. It is important that they be allowed to have their own identities.

SELF ESTEEM

Some hard-of-hearing adults are still struggling today because they did not have the support services they needed when they were children. Some, like me, had to take extra tutoring to do well in college. Some are still feeling socially isolated. Some are still struggling emotionally because of the pain they felt during their earlier years at home, at school or both.

It is so important to build the hard-of-hearing child's self esteem at an early age. One way is to show that adults value communicating with their children. Another way is to focus on a child's strengths and accept the hearing loss as part of the child rather than viewing it as negative. Social behavior can be taught during the toddler and preschool years. We as parents, professionals and others involved in the child's life need to provide the child with a lot of positive experiences. Many hard-of-hearing teenagers that I have counseled struggle with their identities, their hearing aids and social interactions. For some, the problems surface when they are eight or nine years old, but parents think it is just a phase they are going through. We can avoid later problems by providing these students with the skills they need in order to succeed. We need to help them be their own advocates. We want them to think for themselves, to speak out when necessary, enhance their strengths, and be proud of who they are without shame.

Some schools are doing a good job of introducing social skills. The hard-of-hearing students learn how to be accountable for their own behavior, to show appreciation and respect for others, to help others, to express their feelings and understand those of others, to solve problems and conflicts, to handle emotions, to cooperate and listen to others, to learn how to be assertive and to take appropriate risks with adequate support. These skills need to be reinforced on a daily basis.

Hard-of-hearing individuals should not feel scared or intimidated because they have a hearing loss. It is ok if things do not always turn out the way they hope. If I "fall" down, I need to have permission to feel that it is okay. It does not mean that I have failed. I fail if I quit for the wrong reason and do not try again, or if I never try in the first place because of fear. Some parents (and some professionals) always "pick up" their child before he falls down and the child never learns how to take care of himself. For parents to be too over-protective is not good for a child's self image as the child can become emotionally and aca-demically dependent on them. They need to look beyond the hearing loss and see the child's strength and capabilities. They need to help them believe in themselves.

Transition times: from elementary to jun-ior high, from junior high to high school, and from high school to college, are difficult for many hard-of-hearing students. Some hard-of-hearing students who have been in self-contained classrooms during their elementary years can have difficulty adjusting to full mainstreaming in junior high. They miss the warm, familiar environment of a small class-room, their hard-of-hearing friends and their teacher/teacher aides. We need to do a better job of preparing them for each successive stage of their lives.

I don't recall the last time I have been teased. Once in awhile, I will be told by a young child that "I will talk funny." Instead of getting angry, I educate. After I explain why "I talk funny," the young child will normally say, "Oh, okay" and then walk away. The question is not meant to hurt my feelings. It is because the child has never met a hard-of-hearing person before. If I were to react negatively, what would the child learn? I am still hearing comments today about what is happening in the public schools.

Here are seven examples I will share with you:

1. An eight year old hard-of-hearing student has difficulty paying attention in class. As his punishment, he is asked to remove his two hearing aids and give them to his teacher. This is supposed to teach him to pay attention next time.

2. A twelve year old hard-of-hearing student wants her teacher to wear the FM microphone. The teacher refuses to wear it.

3. A high school hard-of-hearing student is told if she fails academically, she will be sent to the state school for the Deaf. Socially, she has many friends. She is doing average work.

4. One teacher reports that her hard-of-hearing students do not need extra support. They are just "lazy" and do not want to learn. Yet some of these students are exhibiting behavior problems.

5.   A six year old hard-of-hearing student requested to take his lunch to school because he can sit in a quiet area. By eating the cafeteria food, he has to sit in the noisy area.

6.   The administrator in a private school will not buy a FM system for a hard-of-hearing student.

7.   A hard-of-hearing junior high student refused to wear her hearing aids because her mother told her she would not get dates in high school.

I have heard these and other comments from parents and professionals working with Deaf/deaf and hard-of-hearing students. They attended my presentations on self esteem that I give throughout the Midwestern, Eastern and Southern United States. There are still teachers who are not trained who do not attend my presentations because they think they do not need it. I realized as years went by, not only as a person who is hard of hearing but as a

professional therapist, that there is still igno-
rance out there.

In the examples mentioned, what could
these teachers and administrators have done
to take the focus off their own convenience
and place it on the needs of the hard-of-hearing students? These student need the same
respect as other students, including equal
access to communication. How can they respect themselves if they are not getting respect from the adults who should be their positive role models?

It is so important for teachers to focus on
the positive. Students need praise. If the
student's work needs to improve, then the
teacher needs to give constructive feedback,
thus helping the child's self image. This is
true for parents as well. It is easier to see and
punish what the child is doing wrong rather
than praising what the child is doing right. It
does not matter if the parents expect appropriate behavior of the child, the child still
needs to hear it. This will allow the child to
keep striving to do better rather than having

the attitude of "I can't do it." The child must feel like a "success" rather than a "failure."

Some classroom teachers do take advantage of opportunities to learn. In 1996, I gave a presentation to 150 regular education teachers. These teachers were not trained to work with Deaf/deaf and hard of hearing students. Their attitudes were positive. They wanted to learn and understand more about hard-of-hearing children. Some traveled a long way to hear me. It was a great feeling for me to see that they cared. I sincerely thanked them for coming. I wish it could happen more often. Their students are fortunate to have them.

As a counselor, I have a good relationship with many wonderful teachers, parents, and other professionals who are dedicated. By working together as a team, this not only makes my job easier, but the students are reaping the benefits of having a strong support system.

Children are our most precious gifts. They are our future. It is our responsibility as parents, administrators, teachers and professionals to see that they do succeed. We should do more than an adequate job. We should do our best!

FINAL THOUGHTS

My purpose for writing this book is to give readers some insights into what it is like to be hard of hearing. For those of you who are hard of hearing, you may have experienced some of the same situations and feelings I have. Others may have their own stories to tell which may be more positive than mine.

As an adult, I still face challenges from time to time. The important thing is to educate rather than give up in frustration. It is easier to avoid situations than confront them. We need to rise above obstacles to show that we CAN. We should never feel shame about who we are. For those of you who have lost your hearing later in life, yes, it can be traumatic. It is not easy to adjust to losing what you once had, your hearing. There are people who have gone through that experience and have made a positive adjustment. Take one small step at a time until you are ready for the next challenge. Do not look back. You can make it happen if you let it happen. It is all up to you! There are supports out there so you do not have to do it alone.

Not too long ago, a fellow worker who is hard of hearing and I came back from lunch and were heading to my office. We heard a strange sound and could not identify it. I asked her if it was her hearing aid whistling but it was much too loud for that. She thought it must be the blower on the ceiling. I already identified that sound and knew it wasn't the blower. We both laughed hard because we looked like two silly fools walking around in my small office trying to locate that noise. We finally traced the noise. My phone was off the hook. As we listened more closely, it made a high, beeping sound. Even after all these years of learning to discriminate noises, we still learn new ones. There are times we make fun of our hearing loss and have a good laugh about it.

How many hard-of-hearing people day-dream during the sermon at church, laugh at jokes without understanding them, or have extra words ready to substitute just in case they mispronounce a word and are asked to repeat themselves? How many times have they been in situations where they take control or avoid a conversation because they are afraid they might misunderstand? But when babies are crying or children are screaming, fans yelling loudly at a football game, a person is whistling, I can tune out the noises and voices I do not want to hear by simply taking off my hearing aids! My problem is once I take them off, I don't always remember where I put them!

Another incident happened to me when I was riding to the airport in a shuttle van. It was dark and I was the only one riding in it. The driver said something and I asked her to please repeat the question. She asked, "What airline?" As often is the case, part of it was guesswork for these are common questions. I told her "United." I looked around and then I heard her talking again. Pretending to understand her, I said "Yeah, yeah" (chuckling a little) a few times. Then I noticed she was talking into a microphone. Of course, I wanted to shrink into my jacket and hide my head. Luckily, she was not paying attention to me. If she had been, she probably would have thought I talked to myself. By being up front about our hearing loss, we can avoid awkward, embarrassing situations. Patience and laughter are two important ingredients I think we all need to apply each day.

There are many assistive devices today that make our lives easier and more adaptable. There are good resources and materials to learn more about hard-of-hearing people. One good resource is "Hearing Loss: The Journal of Self Help for Hard of Hearing People." The journal comes out every two months. For more information, you can contact your local SHHH chapter or contact the national headquarter in Bethesda, Maryland.

I got to where I am today because I made a choice and I took risks. One of the risks is writing this book. I was given support and encouragement by friends and family. However, the final push that I needed was from my first cousin, Bill Dodds, who is a professional writer himself. He, along with his mother, came to my parents' 50th wedding anniversary in July of 1996. After corresponding several times with Bill, he asked me, "Why not you? If you can make a difference in one person's life, then it will be worthwhile to write this book." I agreed!

At my parents' anniversary reception, I visited with relatives and friends of my parents that I had not seen for quite some time. Afterward, it dawned on me that I had strong community support during my childhood years in spite of my school experiences. I realized how blessed I was to have known these people.

As I watched my parents mingled with their relatives and close friends, I was filled with admiration for them. I recalled not too long ago when my mother, along with my two youngest sisters took a sign language class at a local community college. One of my sisters eventually graduated from the same interpreting program that I attended and is an educational interpreter. My mother taught my fa-

ther a few signs. Even though they have forgotten most of the signs because they do not
use them much, they cared enough to want
to learn for me and my brother! My mother
did a song in sign, "The Rose" by Bette Midler,
for her Friday Study Club because she knew I
loved this song. She was very proud! She
gave a presentation on sign language and
handed each member a manual alphabet card.
A sign language book that I gave her lay on
top of her coffee table for many years. What
can I say about this? This is unconditional
love and acceptance. I am truly blessed!

As I mentioned earlier in my book, I
watched my brother many years ago from my
car at the school for the Deaf being surrounded
by Deaf children who loved him. This has
also happened to me. As I was walking into
the school building to provide counseling ser
vices, several hard-of-hearing and deaf students ran up to me and greeted me with hugs
and kind words. They were happy to see me.
Immediately, I felt tears welling up in my eyes
because it was such a wonderful, warm feeling to be loved and to love them back. I can-

not stop counting my blessings.   Thus far, I have learned so much from these beautiful children.

When I was in denial, I did not like where my life was heading. How can I expect others to respect me if I did not respect myself? Therefore, I prayed for guidance. I would never have dreamt that my journey would be as wonderful as it has been for the last 25 years. Part of my success today is being in a positive environment with a supportive staff and having many wonderful friends. They respect me as a person and for the work I do. This instills confidence in me. By showing that confidence, people can see that I feel good about myself and know who I am. Another part of my success is my family members who believed in me. They gave me encouragement, love and support. Without them, I am not sure what would have happened to me! And lastly, my success has to do with believing in myself, the perseverance to continue and not give up with God's help.

Ironically, as an adult, I have the support at work, at home, and in the community to make my life fulfilling. All of us have a journey but where we go is up to us. I pray to God to continue giving me the wisdom to help others believe in themselves so they, too, can fulfill their dreams.

> *"Your attitude can make a difference*
> *in which path you take in life.*
> *Believe in yourself and follow that*
> *path, no matter how long it takes.*
> *It's worth it." Maureen Mann*

FOOTNOTES

[1]When I was in my twenties, I learned that for all these years, I had said the word "giraffe" wrong. It is pronounced with a "j" sound and not a "g" sound. Just recently I learned that "gyro" is pronounced with a "y", not a "g". Can one imagine the hundreds of words that are exceptions to the rules?

[2] The Deaf community has existed for many years. It has a rich cultural history. The community has its own organizations, values, attitudes, residential schools for the Deaf and language which is called "American Sign Language". Deaf people do not view their hearing loss as a disability. They are referred to as "Deaf" with a capital "D". The word "deaf" with a small "d" refer to people who may or may not be involved with the Deaf community. They do not identify themselves as being "culturally Deaf".

REFERENCES

Froehlinger, V. (1981). *Today's Hearing Impaired Child: Into the Mainstream of Education.* The Alexander Graham Bell Association for the Deaf.

Mann, M. (1991). *Adjustment Issues of Hearing-Impaired Adolescents.* Omaha, NE: Boys Town National Research Hospital.

Mann, M. (1995). *Why me? Dealing with Anger.* Bethesda, MD: Self Help for Hard of Hearing People.

SUGGESTIONS FOR TEACHERS IN TEACHING A HARD-OF-HEARING STUDENT IN THE CLASSROOM

- A hard-of-hearing student has the same capabilities and potential as his/her hearing peers. It is important that the student has equal access to learning which is the key to his/her success in the classroom.

- Inservice training should be provided before a hard-of-hearing student is placed in the mainstream to help his/her teachers better understand hearing loss and what impact it has on the student's academic/social needs.

- It is helpful to meet the hard-of-hearing student before he/she enters your class. A teacher can more easily identify strengths and interests of a new student after meeting him/her.

- Educate the class about hearing loss. The hard-of-hearing student may volunteer to discuss this topic, or with the student's permission, invite a hard-of-hearing adult.

- Teach your students how to be responsible in providing good communication/listening skills.

- Before you start talking to a hard-of-hearing student, get his/her attention. It is important to maintain good eye contact.

- Speak in a natural tone of voice when speaking to a hard-of-hearing student. Raising your voice loudly distorts sounds. It also attracts unwanted attention.

- It helps a hard-of-hearing student's attention if the teacher uses facial expressions consistent with verbal messages.

- Keep hands/objects away from your face while speaking.

- Remember it is more difficult to speechread a person with a beard, mustache, or a person who has minimal mouth movement.

- Try to stand close to the hard-of-hearing student you are teaching.

- Try not to stand near a glaring window. This makes lipreading difficult.

- A teacher should not walk around the room or have his/her back to the hard-of-hearing student as this can make communication difficult to follow.

- Be sure that the hard-of-hearing student sits where he/she has access to visual aids and the faces of other students and the teacher.

- Be sure that the hard-of-hearing student is seated as far as possible from noise interference such as the blower, hallway, and near open window.

- Be sensitive to background noises and what you and the class can do to minimize them.

- It is important for the classroom to have good lights. Bad lights can create fatigue and affect the hard-of-hearing student's ability to speechread.

- Visual aids such as blackboards, flip charts, real objects, roleplaying, maps, charts, drawings, pictures, globe, overhead transparencies, software, pc captioning equipment and videotapes/ television with captions help the hard-of-hearing student process information.

- When utilizing audio tapes, a slide projector, television or videotapes that are not open or closed captioned, it would be helpful to give the hard-of-hearing student printed materials on the topic being discussed ahead of time so he/she can follow more readily, and if available, a script of the actual lesson.

- In small or large group activities, be sensitive to the hard-of-hearing student's needs in order to allow him/her to participate successfully.

- Teach the hard-of-hearing student how to appropriately interrupt without embarrassment if he/she does not understand the question, if there is noise interference, and/or if he/she misses a response from a classmate.

- If a hard-of-hearing student is not paying attention, check to see if the problem might not be understanding

the lesson, fatigue or frustration, a dead
hearing aid battery or malfunction FM
or distracting noises.

- Help the hard-of-hearing children attend to information from other children
rather than just the teacher. This will
help them develop classroom discus-
sion and listening skills. They can
also avoid embarrassing themselves by
asking a question already asked by
someone else.

- Often, a hard-of-hearing person may
smile, nod, or act as if the message is
understood even if it is not. It will
be helpful to:

  - Check comprehension by asking
  questions in a non-embarrassing way
  to ensure your listener understood
  what was said.

  - Rephrase your message if you feel you
  are not understood. Do not keep
  repeating the same words.

   - Identify other students speaking in class and repeat or rephrase what they say.

- Provide a good notetaker for the hard-of-hearing student so he/she does not have to worry about missing key information. Select the best notetaker by reviewing the notes of several students.

- When you are giving homework assignments or announcing an upcoming test/quiz, it would be helpful to write the information on the board.

- A hard-of-hearing student needs to be responsible for his/her own homework or tasks assigned to him/her.

- Help the hard-of-hearing student in areas where he/she needs to improve without fostering dependency. Provide enough cues initially to allow the student to experience some success before demanding independence.

- During oral reading time in reading class, it would be helpful to identify the reader by his/her own name and tell him/her how far to read.

- If new vocabulary items or technical words are being used, write them on the board or overhead.

- If a hard-of-hearing student is struggling with English, reading and/or writing, this may be due to limited access to language.

- When you are giving a verbal test, make sure the hard-of-hearing student is following you closely without difficulty.

- If a hard-of-hearing student scores low on a standardized test, this may be due to language barrier, not a reflection of his/her intelligence.

- When a hard-of-hearing student needs to take a standardized test, it should be given by a trained professional with knowledge and expertise in the field of deafness.

- When you are praising the hard-of-hearing student, describe the specific behavior to instill confidence and to foster independence.

- Focus on the hard-of-hearing student's strengths. Daily provide some assignments and activity types where the student easily experiences success. This can enhance the student's self image.

- If a hard-of-hearing student is often alone or isolated, check to see what the concerns may be and how they can be addressed.

- If you are aware that a hard-of-hearing student is being teased or having difficulty making friends, quietly discuss the issue with him/her. Introduce him/her to a guidance counselor. This shows you care.

- If a hard-of-hearing student is utilizing an educational sign language interpreter, look directly at the student when speaking to him/her, not at the interpreter.

- If a hard-of-hearing student is utilizing a sign language interpreter in the classroom, it is essential to check the interpreter's performance. It is important to hire a qualified educational interpreter to allow the hard-of-hearing child to succeed in a regular classroom.

- Remember that for a deaf/Deaf student who signs, sign language provides significantly more information than speechreading which provides only partial information and is most useful for children who have some usable hearing.

- It is important to remember that wearing hearing aids is not the same as wearing glasses.

- It is important to remember that even though a hard-of-hearing student's speech may be good, it does not necessarily follow that his/her hearing is good.

- It is important to remember that good speech does not equate with intelligence.

- It is important to remember that when a hard-of-hearing student makes a mistake or misunderstands, this does not mean he/she is less competent, less intelligent or should be excluded from future responsibilities, activities and opportunities.

- Encourage a hard-of-hearing student to take appropriate risks such as entering spelling contests, joining a debate team or auditioning for a school play if he/she shows an interest. His/her hearing loss should not be a deterrent.

- If the hard-of-hearing child's social-emotional needs are not being met, this should be incorporated in the child's IEP.

- It is important to remember not to "stereotype" Deaf/deaf and hard-of-hearing students. Each one is a unique individual with special talents and personality.

- It is important to have a strong network of people working together as a team to help make the hard-of-hearing student's adjustment into the main-stream setting positive and rewarding. To ensure a successful educational placement, the student needs to succeed both academically and social/emotional.

REFERENCES

1. Lambert, T. (1994). How To Have A Winning Year Teaching The Student Who Is Deaf Or Hard Of Hearing. Washington, D.C.: Alexander Graham Bell Association for the Deaf.

2. Mann, M. (1991). Adjustment Issues of Hearing-Impaired Adolescents, <u>Pediatric Amplification.</u> 173-181. Omaha, NE: Boys Town National Research Hospital.

3. Spinks, D., & Spink, S. (Eds.). (1995). In the Mainstream. Northampton, MA: Clark Mainstream News.

SUGGESTED READINGS

Candlish, P. (1996): *Not Deaf Enough: Raising a Child Who is Hard of Hearing with Hugs, Humor and Imagination.* Washington, D.C. Alexander Graham Bell Association for the Deaf, Inc.

Davis, J. (2003): *Our Forgotten Children: Hard of Hearing Pupils in the Schools* (Rev. 3rd ed.). Bethesda, Maryland.   SHHH publications.

Hearing Loss: The Journal of Self Help for Hard of Hearing People. Bethesda, Maryland: Self Help for Hard of Hearing People.

Mann, M. (1995). Why Me? Dealing with Anger. *Hearing Loss: The Journal of Self Help for Hard of Hearing People.* Bethesda, Maryland: Self Help for Hard of Hearing People.

Marschark, M. (1997). *Raising and Educating a Deaf Child: A Comprehensive Guide to the Choices, Controversies, and Decisions Faced by Parents and Educators.* New York, New York: Oxford University Press.

Padden, Carol & Humphries, Tom. (1988). *Deaf in America: Voice from a Culture.* Cambridge, MA: Harvard University Press.
The Endeavor: A Publication for Families and Professionals Committed to Children who are Deaf or Hard of Hearing. Gettysburg, PA: The American Society for Deaf Children.

SUGGESTED VIDEOTAPE

FAMILIES WITH HARD-OF-HEARING CHILDREN
Developed by the Illinois Educational Audiology Association and produced by the Boys Town National Research Hospital. Omaha, NE: Boys Town Press.

INFORMATION RESOURCES
AND ORGANIZATIONS

1.   ADARA: Professionals Networking
      for Excellence in Service Delivery
      with Individuals who are Deaf/deaf or
      Hard of Hearing
      P.O. Box 727
      Lusby, MO 20657
      http://www.adara.org

2.   Alexander Graham Bell Association
      for the Deaf, Inc.
      3417 Volta Place NW
      Washington, D.C. 20007
      (202) 337-5220 (V)
      (202) 337-5221 (TTY)
      http://www.agbell.org

3.   American Society for Deaf Children
      P.O. Box 3355
      Gettysburg, PA 17325
      (717) 334-7922 (V/TTY)
      (800)942-ASDC (Parent Hotline)
      http://www.asdc@deafchildren.org

4. Association of Late-Deafened Adults
    (ALDA, Inc.)
    1131 Lake St, #204
    Oak Park, IL 60301
    (877) 907-1738 (V/FAX)
    (708) 358-0135 (TTY)
    http://www.alda.org

5. Boys Town National Research Hospital
    555 North 30th Street
    Center for Childhood Deafness
    Omaha, NE 68131
    (402) 498-6696 (V/TTY)
    http://www.boystown.org

6. Captioned Media Program
    National Association of the Deaf
    1447 E. Main Street
    Spartansburg, SC 29307
    (864)585-1778 (V)
    (864)585-2617 (TTY)
    (800) 237-6213 (V)
    (800) 237-6819 (TTY)
    http://www.cfv.org

7.   Cochlear Implant Association, Inc.
      5335 Wisconsin Ave NW, Suite 440
      Washington D.C. 20015-2052
      (202) 895-2781
      http://www.cici.org

8.   Gallaudet University
      800 Florida Avenue NE
      Washington D.C. 20002
      (202) 651-5000 (V/TTY)
      http://www.gallaudet.edu

9.   National Association of the Deaf
      814 Thayer Avenue
      Silver Spring, MD 20910-4500
      (301) 587-1788 (V)
      (301) 587-1789 (TTY)
      http://www.nad.org

10. National Information Center for
      Children and Youth with Disabilities
      P.O. Box 1492
      Washington, D.C. 20013
      (800) 695-0285 (V/TTY)
      http://www.nichcy@aed.org

11. National Theatre of the Deaf
    55 Van Dyke Avenue, Suite 312
    Hartford, CN 06106
    (860) 724-5179 (V/TTY)
    (800) 300-5179 (V/TTY)
    http://www.ntd.org

12. PEPNet (Postsecondary Education
    Programs Network) - A national
    collaboration of four regional post
    secondary education centers for
    individuals who are Deaf/deaf and hard
    of hearing
    http://www.pepnet.org

13. Self Help for Hard of Hearing People,
    Inc. (SHHH)
    7910 Woodmont Avenue, Suite 1200
    Bethesda, MD 20814
    (301) 657-2248 (V)
    (301) 657-2249 (TTY)
    http://www.hearingloss.org

14. TDI National Directory and Resource
     Guide – Promoting Equal access to
     Telecommunications and Media for
     People who are Deaf, Late-Deafened,
     Hard-of-hearing, or Deaf-Blind
     8630 Fenton Street – Suite 604
     Silver Spring, Maryland 20910-3803
     (301)589-3006 (TTY)
     (301)589-3786 (V)
     Info@tdi-online.org
     www.tdi-online.org